Cram101 Textbook Outlines to accompany:

Psychology in Action

Karen Huffman, 9th Edition

PRACTICE EXAMS.

Get all of the self-teaching practice exams for each chapter of this textbook at **www.Cram101.com** and ace the tests. Here is an example:

Chapter 1

Psychology in Action
Karen Huffman, 9th Edition,
All Material Written and Prepared by Cram101

I WANT A BETTER GRADE.   Items 1 - 50 of 100.

1 _____ is any of several traditions or systems in which knowledge of the apparent positions of celestial bodies is held to be useful in understanding, interpreting, and organizing knowledge about human existence.

○ Astrology   ○ A priori
○ Aba reversal design   ○ Abstract principles

2 _____ is the art of characterization and foretelling the future through the study of the palm. The practice is found all over the world, with numerous cultural variations. The practice is regarded by many as a pseudoscience, and no hard scientific evidence has been found to back up claims of veracity.

○ Palmistry   ○ P.E.A.S.
○ P11   ○ P300

3 _____ is the study of human behavior from the point of view of motivation and drives, depending largely on the functional significance of emotion, and based on the assumption that an individual"s total personality and reactions at any given time are the product of the interaction between their conscious/unconscious mind, genetic constitution and their environment.

○ Psychodynamics   ○ P.E.A.S.
○ P11   ○ P300

4 The _____ is the lower part of the brain, adjoining and structurally continuous with the spinal cord. Most sources consider the pons, medulla oblongata, and midbrain all to be part of the _____.

You get a 50% discount for the online exams. Go to **Cram101.com**, click Sign Up at the top of the screen, and enter DK73DW8594 in the promo code box on the registration screen. Access to Cram101.com is $4.95 per month, cancel at any time.

With Cram101.com online, you also have access to extensive reference material.

You will nail those essays and papers. Here is an example from a Cram101 Biology text:

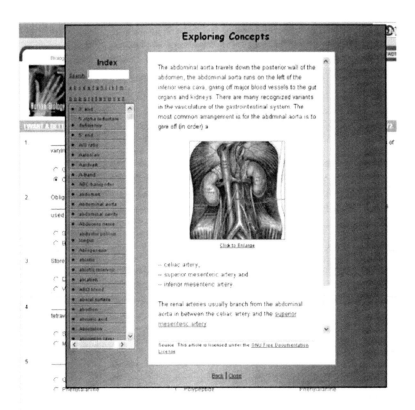

Visit **www.Cram101.com**, click Sign Up at the top of the screen, and enter DK73DW8594 in the promo code box on the registration screen. Access to www.Cram101.com is normally $9.95 per month, but because you have purchased this book, your access fee is only $4.95 per month, cancel at any time. Sign up and stop highlighting textbooks forever.

Learning System

Cram101 Textbook Outlines is a learning system. The notes in this book are the highlights of your textbook, you will never have to highlight a book again.

How to use this book. Take this book to class, it is your notebook for the lecture. The notes and highlights on the left hand side of the pages follow the outline and order of the textbook. All you have to do is follow along while your instructor presents the lecture. Circle the items emphasized in class and add other important information on the right side. With Cram101 Textbook Outlines you'll spend less time writing and more time listening. Learning becomes more efficient.

Cram101.com Online

Increase your studying efficiency by using Cram101.com's practice tests and online reference material. It is the perfect complement to Cram101 Textbook Outlines. Use self-teaching matching tests or simulate in-class testing with comprehensive multiple choice tests, or simply use Cram's true and false tests for quick review. Cram101.com even allows you to enter your in-class notes for an integrated studying format combining the textbook notes with your class notes.

Visit **www.Cram101.com**, click Sign Up at the top of the screen, and enter **DK73DW8594** in the promo code box on the registration screen. Access to www.Cram101.com is normally $9.95 per month, but because you have purchased this book, your access fee is only $4.95 per month. Sign up and stop highlighting textbooks forever.

Psychology in Action
Karen Huffman, 9th

CONTENTS

Astrology	Astrology is any of several traditions or systems in which knowledge of the apparent positions of celestial bodies is held to be useful in understanding, interpreting, and organizing knowledge about human existence.
Palmistry	Palmistry is the art of characterization and foretelling the future through the study of the palm. The practice is found all over the world, with numerous cultural variations. The practice is regarded by many as a pseudoscience, and no hard scientific evidence has been found to back up claims of veracity.
Psychodynamics	Psychodynamics is the study of human behavior from the point of view of motivation and drives, depending largely on the functional significance of emotion, and based on the assumption that an individual"s total personality and reactions at any given time are the product of the interaction between their conscious/unconscious mind, genetic constitution and their environment.
Brain stem	The brain stem is the lower part of the brain, adjoining and structurally continuous with the spinal cord. Most sources consider the pons, medulla oblongata, and midbrain all to be part of the brain stem.
Massed practice	Massed practice refers to learning in one long practice session as opposed to spacing the learning in shorter practice sessions over an extended period.
Biopsychology	Biopsychology is the scientific study of the biological bases of behavior and mental states. Empirical experiments study changes in central nervous system activation in response to a stimulus.
Experimental psychology	Experimental psychology is an approach to psychology that treats it as one of the natural sciences, and therefore assumes that it is susceptible to the experimental method.
Forensic psychology	Psychological research and theory that deals with the effects of cognitive, affective, and behavioral factors on legal proceedings and the law is a forensic psychology.
Industrial/organizational psychology	Industrial/organizational psychology is an applied branch of psychology concerned with behavior of individuals and groups in organizations.
Functionalism	Functionalism was created by William James and influenced by Darwin. This school of psychology focuses on past experience and behavior. It adressed how experience permits people to function better in our environment. According to functionalism, the mental states that make up consciousness can essentially be defined as complex interactions between different functional processes.
Introspection	Introspection is the mental self-observation reporting of conscious inner thoughts, desires and sensations. It is a conscious mental and usually purposive process relying on thinking, reasoning, and examining one"s own thoughts feelings, and, in more spiritual cases, one"s soul. It can also be called contemplation of one"s self, and is contrasted with extrospection, the observation of things external to one"s self. Introspection may be used synonymously with self-reflection and used in a similar way.
Natural selection	Natural selection is a process by which biological populations are altered over time, as a result of the propagation of heritable traits that affect the capacity of individual organisms to survive and reproduce.

Structuralism	The school of psychology that argues that the mind consists of three basic elements senzations, feelings, and images which combine to form experience is structuralism-- a term coined by Titchener. They were associationists in that they believed that complex ideas were made up of simpler ideas that were combined in accordance with the laws of association.
Free will	The idea that human beings are capable of freely making choices or decisions is free will.
Humanistic perspective	The approach that suggests that all individuals naturally strive to grow, develop, and be in control of their lives and behavior is called the humanistic perspective.
Self-actualization	Self-actualization is the instinctual need of humans to make the most of their abilities and to strive to be the best they can. It is the intrinsic growth of what is already in the organism, or more accurately, of what the organism is.
Cognitive psychology	Cognitive psychology is the school of psychology that examines internal mental processes such as problem solving, memory, and language.
Positive psychology	Positive psychology is a relatively young branch of psychology that "studies the strengths and virtues that enable individuals and communities to thrive." Practical applications of positive psychology include helping individuals and organizations correctly identify their strengths and use them to increase and sustain their respective levels of well-being.
Sociocultural perspective	The view that focuses on the roles of ethnicity, gender, culture, and socioeconomic status in personality formation, behavior, and mental processes is a sociocultural perspective.
Applied research	Applied research is done to solve specific, practical questions; its primary aim is not to gain knowledge for its own sake. It can be exploratory but often it is descriptive. It is almost always done on the basis of basic research.
Basic research	Basic research has as its primary objective the advancement of knowledge and the theoretical understanding of the relations among variables . It is exploratory and often driven by the researcher's curiosity, interest or hunch.
Meta-analysis	In statistics, a meta-analysis combines the results of several studies that address a set of related research hypotheses. The first meta-analysis was performed by Karl Pearson in 1904, in an attempt to overcome the problem of reduced statistical power in studies with small sample sizes; analyzing the results from a group of studies can allow more accurate data analysis.
Scientific method	Scientific method refers to the body of techniques for investigating phenomena, acquiring new knowledge, or correcting and integrating previous knowledge. A scientific method consists of the collection of data through observation and experimentation, and the formulation and testing of hypotheses.
Hypothesis	A hypothesis consists either of a suggested explanation for a phenomenon or of a reasoned proposal suggesting a possible correlation between multiple phenomena.
Operational definition	An operational definition is a showing of something—such as a variable, term, or object—in terms of the specific process or set of validation tests used to determine its presence and quantity. Properties described in this manner must be publicly accessible so that persons other than the definer can independently measure or test for them at will. An operational definition is generally designed to model a conceptual definition.

Informed Consent	Informed consent is a legal condition whereby a person can be said to have given consent based upon an appreciation and understanding of the facts and implications of an action.
Comparative psychology	Comparative psychology refers to the study of the behavior and mental life of animals other than human beings. Strictly speaking, comparative psychology ought to involve the use of a comparative method, in which similar studies are carried out on animals of different species, and the results interpreted in terms of their different phylogenetic or ecological backgrounds.
Confidentiality	Confidentiality has been defined by the International Organization for Standardization as "ensuring that information is accessible only to those authorized to have access" and is one of the cornerstones of Information security. Confidentiality is one of the design goals for many cryptosystems, made possible in practice by the techniques of modern cryptography.
Debriefing	A debriefing is a one-time, semi-structured conversation with an individual who has just experienced a stressful or traumatic event. In most cases, the purpose of debriefing is to reduce any possibility of psychological harm by informing people about their experience or allowing them to talk about it.
Randomized controlled trial	A randomized controlled trial is a scientific procedure most commonly used in testing medicines or medical procedures.
Clever Hans	*Clever Hans* was a horse that was claimed to have been able to perform arithmetic and other intellectual tasks. After formal investigation in 1907, psychologist Oskar Pfungst demonstrated that the horse was not actually performing these mental tasks, but was watching the reaction of his human observers. Pfungst discovered this artifact in the research methodology, wherein the horse was responding directly to involuntary cues in the body language of the human trainer, who had the faculties to solve each problem.
Control group	A control group augments integrity in experiments by isolating variables as dictated by the scientific method in order to make a conclusion about such variables. In other cases, an experimental control is used to prevent the effects of one variable from being drowned out by the known, greater effects of other variables. this case, the researchers can either use a control group or use statistical techniques to control for the other variables.
Experiment	In the scientific method, an experiment is a set of observations performed in the context of solving a particular problem or question, to support or falsify a hypothesis or research concerning phenomena. The experiment is a cornerstone in the empirical approach to acquiring deeper knowledge about the physical world.
Experimenter bias	The influence of the experimenter's own expectations or actions on the outcome of the research are called experimenter bias effects.
Dependent variable	The terms Dependent variable and "in Dependent variable " are used in similar but subtly different ways in mathematics and statistics as part of the standard terminology in those subjects. They are used to distinguish between two types of quantities being considered, separating them into those available at the start of a process and those being created by it, where the latter (Dependent variable s) are dependent on the former (in Dependent variable s.)

	The in Dependent variable is typically the variable being manipulated or changed and the Dependent variable is the observed result of the in Dependent variable being manipulated.
Extraneous variables	Extraneous variables are variables other than the independent variable that may bear any effect on the behavior of the subject being studied.
Independent variable	The terms "dependent variable" and Independent variable are used in similar but subtly different ways in mathematics and statistics as part of the standard terminology in those subjects. They are used to distinguish between two types of quantities being considered, separating them into those available at the start of a process and those being created by it, where the latter (dependent variables) are dependent on the former (Independent variable s.) The Independent variable is typically the variable being manipulated or changed and the dependent variable is the observed result of the Independent variable being manipulated.
Ethnocentrism	Ethnocentrism is the tendency to look at the world primarily from the perspective of one's own culture.
Placebo effect	Placebo effect is the term applied by medical science to the therapeutical and healing effects of inert medicines and/or ritualistic or faith healing practices. This effect has been known for years. Generally, one third of a control group taking a placebo shows improvement and Harvard's Herbert Benson says that the placebo effect yields beneficial clinical results in 60–90% of diseases.
Random sampling	The selection of participants in an unbiased manner so that each potential participant has an equal possibility of being selected for the experiment is called random sampling.
Random assignment	Assignment of participants to experimental and control groups by chance is called random assignment. Random assigment reduces the likelihood that the results are due to preexisiting systematic differences between the groups.
Descriptive research	Descriptive research is also known as statistical research. It describes data about the population being studied. Descriptive reseach answers the following questions: who, what, where, when and how.
Naturalistic observation	Naturalistic observation is a method of observation, commonly used by psychologists, behavioral scientists and social scientists, that involves observing subjects in their natural habitats. Researchers take great care in avoiding making interferences with the behavior they are observing by using unobtrusive methods.
Correlational research	Research that examines the relationship between two sets of variables to determine whether they are associated is called correlational research.
Negative correlation	A negative correlation refers to a relationship between two variables in which one variable increases as the other decreases.
Scatterplot	A scatterplot is a graph used in statistics to visually display and compare two or more sets of related quantitative, or numerical, data by displaying only finitely many points, each having a coordinate on a horizontal and a vertical axis.

Radiofrequency lesioning	Radiofrequency lesioning is an outpatient procedure to treat pain, performed most frequently in a fluoroscopy room. Numbing medication is injected followed by a radiofrequency needle at the suspected pain site. After confirmation that the needle tip is positioned correctly, an electrode is inserted into the needle. The proper location is confirmed by fluoroscopy. Using electrical stimulation, the correct nerve is identified by the patient in response to a "tingling" or "buzzing" sensation. This sensation does not typically produce any pain.
Electroencephalography	Electroencephalography is the measurement of electrical activity produced by the brain as recorded from electrodes placed on the scalp.
Brain imaging	Brain imaging is a fairly recent discipline within medicine and neuroscience. Brain imaging falls into two broad categories -- structural imaging and functional imaging.
Magnetic resonance imaging	Magnetic resonance imaging is a non-invasive method used to render images of the inside of an object. It is primarily used in medical imaging to demonstrate pathological or other physiological alterations of living tissues.
Transcranial magnetic stimulation	A Transcranial magnetic stimulation is a noninvasive method to excite neurons in the brain.
Time management	Time management refers to a range of skills, tools, and techniques used to manage time when accomplishing specific tasks, projects and goals. This set encompass a wide scope of activities, and these include planning, allocating, setting goals, delegation, analysis of time spent, monitoring, organizing, scheduling, and prioritizing. Initially Time management referred to just business or work activities, but eventually the term broadened to include personal activities also.
Glial cells	Glial cells are non-neuronal cells that provide support and nutrition, maintain homeostasis, form myelin, and participate in signal transmission in the nervous system.
Axon	An axon is a long, slender projection of a nerve cell, or neuron, that conducts electrical impulses away from the neuron"s cell body or soma.
Soma	The soma is the bulbous end of a neuron, containing the cell nucleus.
Neurotransmitters	Neurotransmitters are chemicals that are used to relay, amplify and modulate signals between a neuron and another cell. There are many different ways to classify neurotransmitters. Often, dividing them into amino acids, peptides, and monoamines is sufficient for many purposes.
Terminal buttons	Terminal buttons are small bulges at the end of axons that send messages to other neurons.
Adrenaline	Adrenaline is a hormone when carried in the blood and a neurotransmitter when it is released across a neuronal synapse. It is a catecholamine, a sympathomimetic monoamine derived from the amino acids phenylalanine and tyrosine.
Dopamine	Dopamine is a hormone and neurotransmitter occurring in a wide variety of animals, including both vertebrates and invertebrates. In the brain, dopamine functions as a neurotransmitter. Dopamine is also a neurohormone released by the hypothalamus. Its main function as a hormone is to inhibit the release of prolactin from the anterior lobe of the pituitary.
Epinephrine	Epinephrine is a hormone and neurotransmitter.

	Epinephrine increases the "fight or flight" response of the sympathetic division of the autonomic nervous system.
	It is a catecholamine, a sympathomimetic monoamine derived from the amino acids phenylalanine and tyrosine.
Gamma aminobutyric acid	Gamma aminobutyric acid is a neurotransmitter that reduces activity across the synapse and thus inhibits a range of behaviors and emotions, especially generalized anxiety.
Norepinephrine	Norepinephrine is a catecholamine and a phenethylamine with chemical formula $C_8H_{11}NO_3$.
Serotonin	Serotonin, is a monoamine neurotransmitter synthesized in serotonergic neurons in the central nervous system and enterochromaffin cells in the gastrointestinal tract of animals including humans. Serotonin is also found in many mushrooms and plants, including fruits and vegetables.
Depolarization	In biology, depolarization is a change in a cell"s membrane potential, making it more positive, or less negative. In neurons and some other cells, a large enough depolarization may result in an action potential. Hyperpolarization is the opposite of depolarization and inhibits the rise of an action potential.
Reuptake	Reuptake is the reabsorption of a neurotransmitter by the neurotransmitter transporter of a pre-synaptic neuron after it has performed its function of transmitting a neural impulse. This prevents further activity of the neurotransmitter, weakening its effects.
Synapse	A synapse is specialized junction through which cells of the nervous system signal to one another and to non-neuronal cells such as muscles or glands. They allow the neurons of the central nervous system to form interconnected neural circuits.
Morphine	Morphine, the principal active agent in opium, is a powerful opioid analgesic drug. According to recent research, it may also be produced naturally by the human brain. Morphine is usually highly addictive, and tolerance and physical and psychological dependence develop quickly.
Cortisol	Cortisol is a corticosteroid hormone produced by the adrenal cortex. It is a vital hormone that is often referred to as the "stress hormone" as it is involved in the response to stress. It increases blood pressure, blood sugar levels and has an immunosuppressive action.
Endocrine system	The endocrine system is an integrated system of small organs which involve the release of extracellular signaling molecules known as hormones. The endocrine system is instrumental in regulating metabolism, growth and development, tissue function, and plays a part also in mood. The field of medicine that deals with disorders of endocrine glands is endocrinology, a branch of the wider field of internal medicine.
Hypothalamus	The hypothalamus is a region of the brain located below the thalamus, forming the major portion of the ventral region of the diencephalon and functioning to regulate certain metabolic processes and other autonomic activities.
Nervous system	The nervous system of an animal coordinates the activity of the muscles, monitors the organs, constructs and also stops input from the senses, and initiates actions.

Peripheral nervous system	The peripheral nervous system consists of the nerves and neurons that serve the limbs and organs. It is not protected by bone or the blood-brain barrier, leaving it exposed to toxins and mechanical injuries. The peripheral nervous system is divided into the somatic nervous system and the autonomic nervous system.
Neurofeedback	Neurofeedback is a therapy technique that presents the user with realtime feedback on brainwave activity, as measured by sensors on the scalp, typically in the form of a video display, sound or vibration. A typical therapy takes 20 to 40 sessions. Some forms of psychotherapy are considerably faster, so neurofeedback is not always the most efficient solution.
Neuroplasticity	Neuroplasticity is the changing of neurons and the organization of their networks and so their function by experience. This idea was first proposed in 1892 by Santiago Ramón y Cajal the proposer of the neuron doctrine though the idea was largely neglected for the next fifty years. The first person to use the term neural plasticity appears to have been the Polish neuroscientist Jerzy Konorski.
Spinal cord	The spinal cord is a thin, tubular bundle of nerves that is an extension of the central nervous system from the brain and is enclosed in and protected by the bony vertebral column. The main function of the spinal cord is transmission of neural inputs between the periphery and the brain.
Stem cell	A Stem Cell is a primal cell that is found in all multi-cellular organisms.
Stroke	In handwriting research, the concept of stroke is used in various ways. In engineering and computer science, there is a tendency to use the term stroke for a single connected component of ink (in Off-line handwriting recognition) or a complete pen-down trace (in on-line handwriting recognition.) Thus, such stroke may be a complete character or a part of a character.
Reflex	A reflex action is an automatic neuromuscular action elicited by a defined stimulus. In most contexts, especially involving humans, a reflex action is mediated via the reflex arc
Autonomic nervous system	The autonomic nervous system is the part of theperipheral nervous system that acts as a control system, maintaining homeostasis in the body. These maintenance activities are primarily performed without conscious control or sensation. . Its most useful definition could be: the sensory and motor neurons that innervate the viscera. These neurons form reflex arcs that pass through the lower brainstem or medulla oblongata.
Babinski reflex	The Babinski reflex is a reflex that can identify disease of the spinal cord and brain and also exists as a primitive reflex in infants.
Primitive reflexes	Primitive reflexes are reflex actions originating in the central nervous system that are exhibited by normal infants but not neurologically in tact adults, in response to particular stimuli. These reflexes disappear or are inhibited by the frontal lobes as a child moves through normal child development.
Parasympathetic nervous system	The parasympathetic nervous system is a division of the autonomic nervous system, along with the sympathetic nervous system and Enteric nervous system. The ANS is a subdivision of the peripheral nervous system.
Somatic nervous system	The somatic nervous system is the part of the peripheral nervous system associated with the voluntary control of body movements through the action of skeletal muscles. The somatic nervous system consists of afferent fibers which receive information from external sources, and efferent fibers which are responsible for muscle contraction.

Sympathetic nervous system	The Sympathetic nervous system is a branch of the autonomic nervous system. It is always active at a basal level and becomes more active during times of stress. Its actions during the stress response comprise the fight-or-flight response. The sympathetic nervous system is responsible for up- and down-regulating many homeostatic mechanisms in living organisms.
Sensory neurons	*Sensory neurons* are neurons that are activated by sensory input (vision, touch, hearing, etc.), and send projections into the central nervous system that convey sensory information to the brain or spinal cord. Unlike neurons of the central nervous system, whose inputs come from other neurons, *Sensory neurons* are activated by physical modalities such as light, sound, temperature, chemical stimulation, etc.
	In complex organisms, *Sensory neurons* relay their information to the central nervous system or in less complex organisms, such as the hydra, directly to motor neurons and *Sensory neurons* also transmit information to the brain, where it can be further processed and acted upon.
Sexual arousal	Sexual arousal is the process and state of an animal being ready for sexual activity. Unlike most animals, human beings of both sexes are potentially capable of sexual arousal throughout the year, therefore, there is no human mating season.
Localization of function	Localization of function is the concept that different parts of the brain serve different, specifiable functions in the control of mental experience and behavior.
Cerebellum	The cerebellum is a region of the brain that plays an important role in the integration of sensory perception and motor output. Many neural pathways link the cerebellum with the motor cortex—which sends information to the muscles causing them to move—and the spinocerebellar tract—which provides feedback on the position of the body in space. The cerebellum integrates these pathways, using the constant feedback on body position to fine-tune motor movements.
Cerebral cortex	The cerebral cortex is a structure within the vertebrate brain with distinct structural and functional properties.
Cerebrum	The cerebrum refers to the cerebral hemispheres and other, smaller structures within the brain. It is the anterior-most embryological division of the brain that develops from the prosencephalon.
Cortex	In anatomy and zoology the cortex is the outermost layer of an organ. Organs with well-defined cortical layers include kidneys, adrenal glands, ovaries, the thymus, and portions of the brain, including the cerebral cortex, the most well-know of all cortices.
Prosencephalon	In the anatomy of the brain of vertebrates, the prosencephalon is the rostral-most portion of the brain. The prosencephalon, the mesencephalon, and rhombencephalon are the three primary portions of the brain during early development of the central nervous system.
Hindbrain	The hindbrain is a developmental categorization of portions of the central nervous system in vertebrates. It can be subdivided in a variable number of transversal swellings called rhombomeres.
Medulla	Medulla refers to the middle of something, and derives from the Latin word for "marrow" In medicine it refers to either bone marrow, the spinal cord, or more generally, the middle part of a structure as opposed to the cortex.

Midbrain	The midbrain is the middle of three vesicles that arise from the neural tube that forms the brain of developing animals. In mature human brains, it becomes the least differentiated, from both its developmental form and within its own structure, among the three vesicles. The midbrain is considered part of the brain stem.
Pons	The pons is a structure located on the brain stem. It is rostral to the medulla oblongata, caudal to the midbrain, and ventral to the cerebellum. In humans and other bipeds this means it is above the medulla, below the midbrain, and anterior to the cerebellum.
Reticular formation	The reticular formation is a part of the brain which is involved in stereotypical actions, such as walking, sleeping, and lying down. It is essential for governing some of the basic functions of higher organisms, and phylogenetically one of the oldest portions of the brain.
Thalamus	An area near the center of the brain involved in the relay of sensory information to the cortex and in the functions of sleep and attention is the thalamus.
Hippocampus	The hippocampus is a part of the brain located in the medial temporal lobe. It forms a part of the limbic system and plays a part in memory and spatial navigation.
Limbic system	The limbic system includes the putative structures in the human brain involved in emotion, motivation, and emotional association with memory. The limbic system influences the formation of memory by integrating emotional states with stored memories of physical sensations.
Motor cortex	Motor cortex is a term that describes regions of the cerebral cortex involved in the planning, control, and execution of voluntary motor functions.
Somatosensory cortex	The primary somatosensory cortex is across the central sulcus and behind the primary motor cortex configured to generally correspond with the arrangement of nearby motor cells related to specific body parts. It is the main sensory receptive area for the sense of touch.
Visual cortex	The term visual cortex refers to the primary visual cortex and extrastriate visual cortical areas such as V2, V3, V4, and V5. The primary visual cortex is anatomically equivalent to Brodmann area 17, or BA17. Brodmann areas are based on a histological map of the human brain created by Korbinian Brodmann.
Corpus callosum	The corpus callosum is a structure of the mammalian brain in the longitudal fissure that connects the left and right cerebral hemispheres. Much of the inter-hemispheric communication in the brain is conducted across the corpus callosum.
Epilepsy	Epilepsy is a chronic neurological condition characterized by recurrent unprovoked neural discharges. It is commonly controlled with medication, although surgical methods are used as well.
Hemispheric specialization	Hemispheric specialization refers to the two hemispheres of the cerebral cortex that are linked by the corpus callosum. Although they have some separate functions, they communicate and coordinate tasks among themselves. The right hemisphere of the cortex performs nonverbal and spatial tasks, whereas the left hemisphere generally dominates speaking and writing functions.

Genetics	Genetics is the science of heredity and variation in living organisms.Knowledge of the inheritance of characteristics has been implicitly used since prehistoric times for improving crop plants and animals through selective breeding. However, the modern science of genetics, which seeks to understand the mechanisms of inheritance, only began with the work of Gregor Mendel in the mid-1800s.
Chromosome	A chromosome is a single large macromolecule of DNA, and constitutes a physically organized form of DNA in a cell. It is a very long, continuous piece of DNA, which contains many genes, regulatory elements and other intervening nucleotide sequences.
Deoxyribonucleic acid	Deoxyribonucleic acid is a nucleic acid that contains the genetic instructions used in the development and functioning of all known living organisms. The main role of DNA molecules is the long-term storage of information and DNA is often compared to a set of blueprints, since it contains the instructions needed to construct other components of cells, such as proteins and RNA molecules.
Gene	A gene is a locatable region of genomic sequence, corresponding to a unit of inheritance, which is associated with regulatory regions, transcribed regions and/or other functional sequence regions.
Polygenic traits	Characteristics that are influenced by more than one pair of genes are referred to as polygenic traits.
Heritability	Heritability It is that proportion of the observed variation in a particular phenotype within a particular population, that can be attributed to the contribution of genotype. In other words: it measures the extent to which differences between individuals in a population are due their being different genetically.
Adoption studies	Research studies that assess hereditary influence by examining the resemblance between adopted children and both their biological and their adoptive parents are referred to as adoption studies. The studies have been inconclusive about the relative importance of heredity in intelligence.
Monozygotic twins	Monozygotic twins derive from a single fertilized egg that divides in two and then goes on to form two separate embryos.
Down syndrome	Down syndrome or is a genetic disorder caused by the presence of all or part of an extra 21st chromosome. Often Down syndrome is associated with some impairment of cognitive ability and physical growth as well as facial appearance. Down syndrome can be identified during pregnancy or at birth.
Family studies	Scientific studies in which researchers assess hereditary influence by examining blood relatives to see how much they resemble each other on a specific trait are called family studies.
Fraternal twins	Fraternal twins usually occur when two fertilized eggs are implanted in the uterine wall at the same time. The two eggs form two zygotes, and these twins are therefore also known as dizygotic as well "biovular" twins. When two eggs are independently fertilized by two different sperm cells, fraternal twins result.
Congenital disorder	A congenital disorder is any medical condition that is present at birth. The term congenital does not imply or exclude a genetic cause. A congenital disorder can be recognized before birth, at birth, or many years later.
Twin	Twin s are a form of multiple birth in which the mother gives birth to two offspring from the same pregnancy, either of the same or opposite sex.

Twin studies	Twin studies are one of a family of designs in behavior genetics which aid the study of individual differences by highlighting the role of environmental and genetic causes on behavior. Modern twin studies have shown that almost all traits are in part influenced by genetic differences, with some characteristics showing a strong influence, others an intermediate level, and some more complex heritabilities, with evidence for different genes affecting different elements of the trait - for instance autism.
Evolutionary psychology	Evolutionary psychology is a theoretical approach to psychology that attempts to explain mental and psychological traits—such as memory, perception, or language—as adaptations, i.e., as the functional products of natural selection.
Social Readjustment Rating Scale	Holmes and Rahe's social readjustment rating scale ranks 43 life events from most to least stressful and assigns a point value to each.
Eustress	Selye called negative stress distress and positive stress eustress.
Burnout	Burnout is a psychological term for the experience of long-term exhaustion and diminished interest, usually in the work context. It is also used as an English slang term to mean exhaustion.
Chronic stress	Chronic stress is stress that lasts a long time or occurs frequently. Chronic stress is potentially damaging. Family problems, a difficult class at school, a schedule that is too busy, or a long illness can cause chronic stress.
Role conflict	Role conflict is a conflict among the roles corresponding to two or more statuses.
Life change units	Life change units are numerical values assigned to each life event on the SRRS.
Approach-approach conflict	A type of conflict in which the goals that produce opposing motives are positive and within reach is referred to as an approach-approach conflict.
Avoidance-avoidance conflict	A type of conflict in which the goals are negative, but avoidance of one requires approaching the other is an avoidance-avoidance conflict.
Frustration	Frustration is an emotion that occurs in situations where one is blocked from reaching a personal goal. The more important the goal, the greater the frustration. It is comparable to anger.
Approach-avoidance conflict	Approach-avoidance conflict refers to the tension experienced by people when they are simultaneously attracted to and repulsed by the same goal.
Homeostasis	Homeostasis is the property of either an open system or a closed system, especially a living organism, which regulates its internal environment so as to maintain a stable, constant condition.
Hypercortisolism	Hypercortisolism is an endocrine disorder caused by high levels of cortisol in the blood from a variety of causes, including primary pituitary adenoma known as Cushing"s disease, primary adrenal hyperplasia or neoplasia, ectopic ACTH production e.g., from a small cell lung cancer, and iatrogenic steroid use.
Adrenal insufficiency	In medicine, adrenal insufficiency is the inability of the adrenal gland to produce adequate amounts of cortisol in response to stress.

Startle reflex	Startle reflex is the response of mind and body to a sudden unexpected stimulus, such as a flash of light, a loud noise, or a quick movement near the face. In human beings, the reaction includes physical movement away from the stimulus, a contraction of the muscles of the arms and legs, and often blinking.
Psychoneuroimmunology	Psychoneuroimmunology is the study of the interaction between psychological processes and the nervous and immune systems of the human body. PNI has an interdisciplinary approach, interlacing disciplines as psychology, neuroscience, immunology, physiology, pharmacology, psychiatry, behavioral medicine, infectious diseases, endocrinology, rheumatology and others.
Natural killer cells	Natural killer cells are a form of cytotoxic lymphocyte which constitute a major component of the innate immune system. NK cells play a major role in the rejection of tumors and virally infected cells. NK cells kill by releasing small cytoplasmic granules of perforin and granzyme that cause the target cell to die by apoptosis. They were named "natural killers" because of the initial notion that they do not require activation in order to kill cells that are "missing self" markers of MHC class I.
Acute stress over reaction	Acute stress over reaction is a psychological condition arising in response to a terrifying event. It should not be confused with the unrelated circulatory condition of shock. "Acute stress response" was first described by Walter Cannon in the 1920s as a theory that animals react to threats with a general discharge of the sympathetic nervous system.
Health psychology	Health psychology concerns itself with understanding how biology, behavior, and social context influence health and illness
Binge drinking	The British Medical Association states that "there is no consensus on the definition of drinking. In the past, " binge drinking " was often used to refer to an extended period of time, usually two days or more, during which a person repeatedly drank to intoxication, giving up usual activities."
Chronic pain	Chronic pain was originally defined as pain that has lasted 6 months or longer. More recently it has been defined as pain that persists longer than the temporal course of natural healing that is associated with a particular type of injury or disease process.
Electromyography	Electromyography is a technique for evaluating and recording physiologic properties of muscles at rest and while contracting.
Problem-focused coping	Lazarus' problem-focused coping is a strategy used by individuals who face their troubles and try to solve them.
Stress management	Stress management encompasses techniques intended to equip a person with effective coping mechanisms for dealing with psychological stress, with stress defined as a person"s physiological response to an internal or external stimulus that triggers the fight-or-flight response.
Procrastination	Procrastination is a type of avoidance behavior which is characterized by deferment of actions or tasks to a later time. It is often cited by psychologists as a mechanism for coping with the anxiety associated with starting or completing any task or decision. The psychological causes of procrastination vary greatly, but generally surround issues of anxiety, low sense of self-worth and a self-defeating mentality.

Bottom-up process	In perception theory, a bottom-up process is a mental procedure that brings the features of the individual stimulus recorded by the senses together to form a perception of larger objects or scenery.
Coding	In sensation, Coding is the process by which information about the quality and quantity of a stimulus is preserved in the pattern of action potentials sent through sensory neurons to the central nervous system.
Synesthesia	Synesthesia is a neurologically based phenomenon in which stimulation of one sensory or cognitive pathway leads to automatic, involuntary experiences in a second sensory or cognitive pathway. Synesthesia is also sometimes reported by individuals under the influence of psychedelic drugs, after a stroke, or as a consequence of blindness or deafness.
Transduction	Tranduction is the transformation of one form of energy to another. In psychology, transduction refers to the nervous system. In the nervous system, transduction occurs when environmental energy is transformed into electrical or neural energy.
Absolute threshold	Absolute threshold is the statistically determined minimum level of stimulation necessary to excite a perceptual system.
Difference threshold	Difference threshold refers to the minimal difference in intensity required between two sources of energy so that they will be perceived as being different 50 percent of the time.
JND	In psychophysics, a just noticeable difference, customarily abbreviated with lowercase letters as *jnd*, is the smallest difference in a specified modality of sensory input that is detectable by a human being. It is also known as the difference limen or the differential threshold. For many sensory dimensions, the "*jnd*" is an increasing function of the base level of input, and the ratio of the two is roughly constant (that is the *jnd* is a constant proportion/percentage of the reference level.)
Just noticeable difference	In psychophysics, a *Just noticeable difference*, is the smallest difference in a specified modality of sensory input that is detectable by a human being. It is also known as the difference limen or the differential threshold. For many sensory dimensions, the "jnd" is an increasing function of the base level of input, and the ratio of the two is roughly constant (that is the jnd is a constant proportion/percentage of the reference level.)
Psychophysics	Psychophysics refers to the study of the mathematical relationship between the physical aspects of stimuli and our psychological experience of them.
Subliminal perception	Subliminal perception is a signal or message embedded in another object, designed to pass below the normal limits of perception. These messages are indiscernible by the conscious mind, but allegedly affect the subconscious or deeper mind.
Tachistoscope	A tachistoscope is a device that displays an image for a specific amount of time. It can be used to increase recognition speed, to show something too fast to be consciously recognized, or to test which elements of an image are memorable.

Acupuncture	Whether acupuncture is efficacious or a placebo is subject to scientific research. Scientists have conducted reviews of existing clinical trials according to the protocols of evidence-based medicine; some have found efficacy for headache, low back pain and nausea, but for most conditions have concluded that there is insufficient evidence to determine whether or not acupuncture is effective.
Gate-control theory	The gate-control theory of pain, put forward by Ron Melzack and Patrick Wall in 1962, is the idea that pain is not a direct result of activation of pain receptor neurons, but rather its perception is modulated by interaction between different neurons.
Sensory adaptation	Sensory adaptation is a change over time in the responsiveness of the sensory system to a constant stimulus. It is usually experienced as a change in the stimulus.
Blindness	Blindness is the condition of lacking visual perception due to physiological or neurological factors.
Phantom pain	Phantom pain is pain that is felt in a part of the body that either no longer exists due to amputation or is insensate as a result of nerve severance.
Substance P	In neuroscience, Substance P is a neuropeptide: a short-chain polypeptide that functions as a neurotransmitter and as a neuromodulator. It belongs to the tachykinin neuropeptide family.
Tinnitus	Tinnitus, "ringing ears" or ear noise is a phenomenon of the nervous system connected to the ear, characterized by perception of a ringing, beating or roaring sound (often perceived as sinusoidal) with no external source.
Lens	The lens is a transparent, biconvex structure in the eye that, along with the cornea, helps to refract light to be focused on the retina. Its function is thus similar to a human-made optical lens. The lens is also known as the aquula or crystalline lens.
Accommodation	Accommodation can be understood as the mechanism by which failure leads to learning: when we act on the expectation that the world operates in one way and it violates our expectations, we often fail, but by accommodation of this new experience and reframing our model of the way the world works, we learn from the experience of failure, or others" failure.
Hyperopia	Hyperopia is a defect of vision caused by an imperfection in the eye, causing inability to focus on near objects, and in extreme cases causing a sufferer to be unable to focus on objects at any distance.
Myopia	Myopia is a refractive defect of the eye in which collimated light produces image focus in front of the retina when accommodation is relaxed. Those with myopia see nearby objects clearly but distant objects appear blurred. With myopia, the eyeball is too long, or the cornea is too steep, so images are focused in the vitreous inside the eye rather than on the retina at the back of the eye.
Nearsightedness	A vision deficiency in which close objects are seen clearly but distant objects appear blurry is nearsightedness.
Presbyopia	Presbyopia is the eye"s diminished ability to focus that occurs with aging. The most widely held theory is that it arises from the loss of elasticity of the crystalline lens, although changes in the lens"s curvature from continual growth and loss of power of the ciliary muscles have also been postulated as its cause. It is not a disease as such, but a condition that affects everyone at a certain age.

Color vision	Color vision is the capacity of an organism or machine to distinguish objects based on the wavelengths of the light they reflect or emit. The nervous system derives color by comparing the responses to light from the several types of cone photoreceptors in the eye.
Dark adaptation	Dark adaptation is the tendency for the peak sensitivity of the human eye to shift toward the blue end of the color spectrum at low illumination levels.
Light adaptation	The process whereby the eyes become less sensitive to light in high illumination is light adaptation.
Opponent-process theory	The opponent-process theory is a color theory that states that the human visual system interprets information about color by processing signals from cones in an antagonistic manner.
Trichromatic theory	The trichromatic theory was postulated by Young and later by Helmholtz. They demonstrated that most colors can be matched by superimposing three separate light sources known as primaries; a process known as additive mixing. The Young-Helmholtz theory of color vision was built around the assumption of there being three classes of receptors.
Primary colors	Primary colors are sets of colors that can be combined to make a useful range of colors. For human applications, three are often used; for additive combination of colors, as in overlapping projected lights or in CRT displays, the Primary colors normally used are red, green, and blue. For subtractive combination of colors, as in mixing of pigments or dyes, such as in printing, the primaries normally used are cyan, magenta, and yellow.
Audition	An Audition is a sample performance by an actor, singer, musician, dancer or other performer. It involves the performer displaying their talent through a previously-memorized and rehearsed solo piece: for example, a monologue for actors or a song for a singer. Used in the context of performing arts, it is analogous to job interviews in many ways.
Auditory nerve	The vestibulocochlear nerve is the eighth of twelve cranial nerves, and also known as the auditory nerve. It is the nerve along which the sensory cells (the hair cells) of the inner ear transmit information to the brain. It consists of the cochlear nerve, carrying information about hearing, and the vestibular nerve, carrying information about balance.
Incus	The incus is a small bone or ossicle in the middle ear. It connects the malleus to the stapes. The incus only exists in mammals, and is derived from a reptilian upper jaw bone, the quadrate bone.
Malleus	The malleus is hammer-shaped small bone or ossicle of the middle ear which connects with the incus and is attached to the inner surface of the eardrum.
Stapes	The stapes is the small bone or ossicle in the middle ear which attaches the incus to the fenestra ovalis, the "oval window" which is adjacent to the vestibule of the inner ear. It is the smallest and lightest bone in the human body.
Tympanic membrane	The tympanic membrane, colloquially known as eardrum, is a thin membrane that separates the outer ear from the middle ear. Its function is to transmit sound from the air to the ossicles inside the middle ear.
Basilar membrane	The basilar membrane within the cochlea of the inner ear is the part of the auditory system that decomposes incoming auditory signals into their frequency components. This allows higher neural processing of sound information to focus on the frequency spectrum of input, rather than just the time domain waveform.

Loudness	Loudness is the quality of a sound that is the primary psychological correlate of physical intensity. Loudness is often approximated by a power function with an exponent of 0.6 when plotted vs. sound pressure or 0.3 when plotted vs. sound intensity.
Nerve deafness	Deafness caused by damage to the hair cells or auditory nerve is nerve deafness.
Timbre	The distinctive quality of a sound that distinguishes it from other sounds of the same pitch and loudness is called timbre.
Absolute pitch	Absolute pitch , widely referred to as perfect pitch, is the ability of a person to identify or recreate a musical note without the benefit of an external reference.
	Absolute pitch, or perfect pitch, is the ability to name or reproduce a tone without reference to an external standard.
Chemical senses	Chemical senses include smell and taste.
Glutamate	Glutamate is one of the 20 standard amino acids used by all organisms in their proteins. It is critical for proper cell function, but it is not an essential nutrient in humans because it can be manufactured from other compounds.
Pheromone	A pheromone is a chemical that triggers a natural behavioral response in another member of the same species.
Taste buds	Taste buds are small structures on the upper surface of the tongue, soft palate, upper esophagus and epiglottis that provide information about the taste of food being eaten. These structures are involved in detecting the five elements of taste perception: salty, sour, bitter, sweet, and umami (or savory.) Via small openings in the tongue epithelium, called taste pores, parts of the food dissolved in saliva come into contact with the taste receptors.
Umami	Umami is one of the five basic tastes sensed by specialized receptor cells present on the human tongue. Umami applies to the sensation of savoriness¡ªspecifically, to the detection of glutamates, which are especially common in meats, cheese and other protein-heavy foods.
Olfactory bulb	The olfactory bulb is a structure of the vertebrate forebrain involved in olfaction, the perception of odors.
Olfactory epithelium	The olfactory epithelium is a specialized epithelial tissue inside the nasal cavity that is involved in smell. The tissue is made of three types of cells: the olfactory receptor neurons which transduce the odor to electrical signals, the supporting cells which protect the neurons and secrete mucus, and the basal cells which are a type of stem cell that differentiate into olfactory receptor neurons to replace dead receptor neurons.
Skin senses	The skin senses include touch, pressure, temperature and pain.
Braille	The braille system, devised in 1821 by Frenchman Louis Braille, is a method that is widely used by blind people to read and write. Each braille character or cell is made up of six dot positions, arranged in a rectangle containing two columns of three dots each.
Kinesthesia	Kinesthesia is the sense of the position of parts of the body, relative to other neighboring parts of the body. Kinesthesia is a sense that provides feedback solely on the status of the body internally.

Motion sickness	Motion sickness is a condition in which a disagreement exists between visually perceived movement and the vestibular system"s sense of movement.
Semicircular canals	The semicircular canals are three half-circular, interconnected tubes located inside each ear that are the equivalent of three gyroscopes located in three planes perpendicular (at right angles) to each other.
Vestibular sense	Vestibular sense is the sensory system that provides the dominant input about our movement and orientation in space. Together with the cochlea, the auditory organ, it is situated in the vestibulum in the inner ear.
Attention	Attention is the cognitive process of selectively concentrating on one aspect of the environment while ignoring other things. Examples include listening carefully to what someone is saying while ignoring other conversations in the room or listening to a cell phone conversation while driving a car.
Homosexuality	Homosexuality refers to a sexual orientation characterized by aesthetic attraction, romantic love, and sexual desire exclusively for members of the same sex or gender identity.
Muller-Lyer illusion	The Muller-Lyer illusion is an optical illusion consisting of nothing more than an arrow. When viewers are asked to place a mark on the figure at the mid-point, they invariably place it more towards the "tail" end. Another variation consists of two arrow-like figures, one with both ends pointing in, and the other with both ends pointing out. When asked to judge the lengths of the two lines, which are equal, viewers will typically claim that the line with outward pointing arrows is longer.
Habituation	In psychology, habituation is an example of non-associative learning in which there is a progressive diminution of behavioral response probability with repetition of a stimulus.
Prosopagnosia	Prosopagnosia is a disorder of face perception where the ability to recognize faces is impaired, while the ability to recognize other objects may be relatively intact. The term usually refers to a condition following acute brain damage, but recent evidence suggests that a congenital form of the disorder may exist. The specific brain area usually associated with Prosopagnosia is the fusiform gyrus.
Gestalt psychology	Gestalt psychology is a theory of mind and brain that proposes that the operational principle of the brain is holistic, parallel, and analog, with self-organizing tendencies; or, that the whole is different than the sum of its parts. The classic Gestalt example is a soap bubble, whose spherical shape is not defined by a rigid template, or a mathematical formula, but rather it emerges spontaneously by the parallel action of surface tension acting at all points in the surface simultaneously.
Reversible figure	A reversible figure is a drawing that is compatible with two different perceptual interpretations that can shift back and forth. It is demonstration of perceptual ambiguity.
Depth perception	Depth perception is the visual ability to perceive the world in three dimensions. It is a trait common to many higher animals. Depth perception allows the beholder to accurately gauge the distance to an object.
Perceptual constancy	Perceptual constancy is the perception of an object or quality as constant under changing conditions.
Brightness constancy	The tendency to perceive an object as being just as bright even though lighting conditions change its physical intensity is called brightness constancy.

Color constancy	*Color constancy* is an example of subjective constancy and a feature of the human color perception system which ensures that the perceived color of objects remains relatively constant under varying illumination conditions. A green apple for instance looks green to us at midday, when the main illumination is white sunlight, and also at sunset, when the main illumination is red. This helps us identify objects.
Shape constancy	The tendency to perceive an object as being the same shape although the retinal image varies in shape as it rotates, is shape constancy.
Size constancy	The tendency to perceive an object as being the same size even as the size of its retinal image changes according to the object's distance is referred to as size constancy.
Visual cliff	An apparatus used to test depth perception in infants and young animals is the visual cliff. Infants, 6-14 months, were placed on the edge of the visual cliff, a small cliff with a drop-off covered by glass, to see if they would crawl over the edge. Most infants refused to crawl out on the glass signifying that they could perceive depth and that depth perception is not learned.
Retinal disparity	A binocular cue for depth based on the difference in the image cast by an object on the retinas of the eyes as the object moves closer or farther away, is called retinal disparity.
Aerial perspective	Aerial perspective is the effect on the appearance of an object by air between it and a viewer. As the distance between an object and a viewer increases, the contrast between the object and its background decreases. The contrast of any markings or details on the object also decreases.
Interposition	Interposition refers to an asserted right of U.S. states to protect their individual interests from federal violation or any abridgement of states" rights deemed by those states to be dangerous or unconstitutional.
Motion parallax	A monocular cue for depth, motion parallax is the apparent relative motion of several stationary objects against a background when the observer moves gives hints about their relative distance. This effect can be seen clearly when driving in a car, nearby things pass quickly, while far off objects appear stationary.
Relative size	Relative size is a monocular cue where an an automobile that is close to us seems larger than one that is far away. The visual system exploits the relative size of similar (or familiar) objects to judge distance.
Texture gradient	Texture gradient is a monocular cue for depth based on the perception that closer objects appear to have rougher surfaces. Objects appear denser as they go further away.
Clairvoyance	Clairvoyance is a purported form of extra-sensory perception that allows a person to perceive distant objects, persons, or events, including "seeing" through opaque objects and the detection of types of energy not normally perceptible to humans.
Extra-sensory perception	Extra-Sensory Perception is defined as ability to acquire information by paranormal means independent of any known physical senses or deduction from previous experience. The term was coined by Duke University researcher J. B. Rhine to denote psychic abilities such as telepathy, precognition and clairvoyance.
Precognition	The purported ability to accurately predict future events is precognition.

Telepathy	Telepathy is the claimed innate ability of humans and other creatures to communicate information from one mind to another, without the use of extra tools such as speech or body language.
Zener cards	Zener cards are cards used to conduct experiments for extra-sensory perception (ESP), most often clairvoyance.
Fallacy of positive instances	The tendency to remember or notice information that fits one's expectations, while forgetting discrepancies, is referred to as the fallacy of positive instances.
Consciousness	The awareness of the sensations, thoughts, and feelings being experienced at a given moment is called consciousness.
Anterograde amnesia	Anterograde amnesia is a form of amnesia, or memory loss; in which new events are not transferred from short-termed memory to long-term memory. This may be a permanent deficit, or it may be temporary, such as is sometimes seen for a period of hours or days after head trauma or for a period of intoxication with an amnestic drug.
Subconscious	The term Subconscious is used in many different contexts and has no single or precise definition. This greatly limits its significance as a meaning-bearing concept, and in consequence the word tends to be avoided in academic and scientific settings. In everyday speech and popular writing, however, the term is very commonly encountered.
Unconscious mind	The unconscious mind refers to information processing and brain functioning of which a person is unaware. In Freudian theory, it is the repository of unacceptable thoughts and feelings.
Melatonin	Melatonin is a hormone found in all living creatures from algae to humans, at levels that vary in a daily cycle. It plays a role in the regulation of the circadian rhythm of several biological functions.
Suprachiasmatic nucleus	The suprachiasmatic nucleus is in the hypothalamus and is so named because it resides immediately above the optic chaism. Its principal function is to create the circadian rhythm, which regulates the body functions over the 24-hour period.
Jet lag	Jet lag is a physiological condition which is a consequence of alterations to the circadian rhythm. The condition of jet lag generally lasts many days or more, and medical experts have deemed that a recovery rate of "one day per time zone" is a fair guideline. The condition is generally believed to be the result of disruption of the "light/dark" cycle that entrains the body"s circadian rhythm. It can be exacerbated by environmental factors.
Sleep deprivation	Sleep deprivation is a general lack of the necessary amount of sleep. This may occur as a result of sleep disorders, active choice or deliberate inducement such as in interrogation or for torture..
Rapid eye movement sleep	Rapid eye movement sleep is the normal stage of sleep characterized by rapid movements of the eyes. Criteria for Rapid eye movement sleep include not only rapid eye movements, but also low muscle tone and a rapid, low voltage EEG these features are easily discernible in a polysomnogram, the sleep study typically done for patients with suspected sleep disorders.
Dyssomnias	Dyssomnias are a broad classification of sleeping disorder that make it difficult to get to sleep, or to stay sleeping.

Insomnia	Insomnia is a sleep disorder characterized by an inability to sleep and/or inability to remain asleep for a reasonable period.
Cataplexy	Sudden loss of muscle tone that accompanies narcolepsy is called cataplexy.
Narcolepsy	A serious sleep disorder characterized by excessive daytime sleepiness and sudden, uncontrollable attacks of REM sleep is called narcolepsy.
Sleep apnea	Sleep apnea refers to a sleep disorder involving periods during sleep when breathing stops and the person must awaken briefly in order to breathe; major symptoms are excessive daytime sleepiness and loud snoring.
Night terror	A night terror is a parasomnia sleep disorder characterized by extreme terror and a temporary inability to regain full consciousness. The subject wakes abruptly from slow-wave sleep, with waking usually accompanied by gasping, moaning, or screaming.
Parasomnias	Parasomnias are a category of sleep disorders that involve abnormal and unnatural movements, behaviors, emotions, perceptions, and dreams that occur while falling asleep, sleeping, between sleep stages, or arousal from sleep. Most Parasomnias are dissociated sleep states which are partial arousals during the transitions between wakefulness and NREM sleep, or wakefulness and REM sleep. NREM Parasomnias are arousal disorders that occur during stages 3 and 4 of NREM sleep--also known as slow wave sleep (SWS.)
Sleeptalking	Speaking that occurs during NREM sleep is called sleeptalking.
Sleepwalking	Sleepwalking is a sleep disorder where the sufferer engages in activities that are normally associated with wakefulness while he or she is asleep or in a sleeplike state. Sleepwalking is more commonly experienced in people with high levels of stress, anxiety or other psychological factors and in people with genetic factors or sometimes a combination of both.
Addiction	The term Addiction is used in many contexts to describe an obsession, compulsion such as: drug Addiction (e.g. alcoholism), video game Addiction crime, money, work Addiction compulsive overeating, problem gambling, computer Addiction nicotine Addiction pornography Addiction etc. In medical terminology, an Addiction is a chronic neurobiologic disorder that has genetic, psychosocial, and environmental dimensions and is characterized by one of the following: the continued use of a substance despite its detrimental effects, impaired control over the use of a drug (compulsive behavior), and preoccupation with a drug"s use for non-therapeutic purposes (i.e. craving the drug.) Addiction is often accompanied the presence of deviant behaviors (for instance stealing money and forging prescriptions) that are used to obtain a drug.
Antagonist drugs	Medications that block or counteract the effects of psychoactive or other drugs are called antagonist drugs.
Cross-tolerance	Cross-tolerance refers to condition in which a person may replace addiction to one drug with addiction to the other when the two drugs have similar chemical makeup and act on the same neurotransmitter receptors.

Drug abuse	Drug abuse has a wide range of definitions related to taking a psychoactive drug or performance enhancing drug for a non-therapeutic or non-medical effect.
Drug addiction	Drug addiction is considered a pathological state. The disorder of addiction involves the progression of acute drug use to the development of drug-seeking behavior, the vulnerability to relapse, and the decreased, slowed ability to respond to naturally rewarding stimuli.
Caffeine	Caffeine is a xanthine alkaloid compound that acts as a psychoactive stimulant in humans. In humans, caffeine is a central nervous system stimulant, having the effect of temporarily warding off drowsiness and restoring alertness. Beverages containing caffeine, such as coffee, tea, soft drinks and energy drinks enjoy great popularity; caffeine is the world"s most widely consumed psychoactive substance, but unlike most other psychoactive substances, it is legal and unregulated in nearly all jurisdictions.
Depressants	Depressants are psychoactive drugs which temporarily diminish the function or activity of a specific part of the body or mind. Examples of these kinds of effects may include anxiolysis, sedation, and hypotension. Due to their effects typically having a "down" quality to them, depressants are also occasionally referred to as "downers".
Stimulants	Stimulants are drugs that temporarily increase alertness and awareness. They usually have increased side-effects with increased effectiveness, and the more powerful variants are therefore often prescription medicines or illegal drugs.
Crack	Crack is a highly addictive form of cocaine that is popular for its intense high. It is a freebase form of the drug that is made using baking soda in a process to convert cocaine hydrochloride into freebase cocaine. When large amounts of dopamine are released by crack consumption, it becomes easier for the brain to generate motivation for other activities.
Hallucinogens	The general group of pharmacological agents commonly known as Hallucinogens can be divided into three broad categories: psychedelics, dissociatives, and deliriants. These classes of psychoactive drugs have in common that they can cause subjective changes in perception, thought, emotion and consciousness.
Opiates	A group of narcotics derived from the opium poppy that provide a euphoric rush and depress the nervous system are referred to as opiates.
Lysergic acid diethylamide	Lysergic acid diethylamide, is a semisynthetic psychedelic drug. It is synthesized from lysergic acid derived from ergot, a grain fungus that typically grows on rye. Many clinical trials were conducted on the potential use of it in psychedelic psychotherapy, generally with very positive results.
Marijuana	Marijuana is the dried vegetable matter of the Cannabis sativa plant. It contains large concentrations of compounds that have medicinal and psychoactive effects when consumed, usually by smoking or eating.
Club drug	A club drug is loosely defined as a faux-category of recreational drugs which are associated with use at dance clubs, parties, and raves.
Date rape drug	Date rape drug refers to any drug which can be used to assist in the commission of a sexual assault. These drugs commonly have sedative, hypnotic, dissociative and/or amnesiac affects, and when used to facilitate rape are often added to a food or drink without the victim"s knowledge.

Methylenedioxymethamphetamine	Methylenedioxymethamphetamine is a semisynthetic entactogen of the phenethylamine family. It is considered a recreational drug, and has long had a strong association with the rave culture. Some scientists have suggested that it may facilitate self-examination with reduced fear, which may prove useful in some therapeutic settings.
Ketamine	Ketamine is a dissociative anesthetic for use in human and veterinary medicine developed by Parke-Davis. Pharmacologically, ketamine is classified as an NMDA receptor antagonist, and, like other drugs of this class such as tiletamine, and phencyclidine, induces a state referred to as "dissociative anesthesia." As with other pharmaceuticals of this type, ketamine is used illicitly as a recreational drug.
MDMA	MDMA, most commonly known today by the street name ecstasy, is a synthetic entactogen of the phenethylamine family whose primary effect is to stimulate the secretion of large amounts of serotonin as well as dopamine and noradrenaline in the brain, causing a general sense of openness, empathy, energy, euphoria, and well-being.
Methamphetamine	Methamphetamine is a psychostimulant and sympathomimetic drug. The dextrorotatory isomer dextromethamphetamine can be prescribed to treat attention-deficit hyperactivity disorder, though unmethylated amphetamine is more commonly prescribed.
Flunitrazepam	Flunitrazepam is a powerful hypnotic drug that is a benzodiazepine derivative. It has powerful hypnotic, sedative, anxiolytic, and skeletal muscle relaxant properties. The drug is sometimes used as a date rape drug. It is a preferred benzodiazepine in chronic users of benzodiazepines with a chronic and massive drug usage.
Meditation	Meditation usually refers to a state in which the body is consciously relaxed and the mind is allowed to become calm and focused.
Hypnosis	*Hypnosis* is a mental state (state theory) or set of attitudes (nonstate theory) usually induced by a procedure known as a hypnotic induction, which is commonly composed of a series of preliminary instructions and suggestions. Hypnotic suggestions may be delivered by a hypnotist in the presence of the subject ("hetero-suggestion"), or may be self-administered ("self-suggestion" or "autosuggestion".) The use of hypnotism for therapeutic purposes is referred to as "hypnotherapy".
Conditioned stimulus	A previously neutral stimulus that elicits the conditioned response because of being repeatedly paired with a stimulus that naturally elicited that response, is called a conditioned stimulus.
Neutral stimulus	Neutral stimulus is a stimulus which initially produces no specific response other than focusing attention. In classical conditioning, when used together with an unconditioned stimulus, the neutral stimulus becomes a conditioned stimulus.
Unconditioned response	An Unconditioned Response is the response elicited to an unconditioned stimulus. It is a natural, automatic response.
Unconditioned stimulus	In classical conditioning, an unconditioned stimulus elicits a response from an organism prior to conditioning. It is a naturally occurring stimulus and a naturally occurring response..

Behaviorism	Behaviorism is a philosophy of psychology based on the proposition that all things which organisms do including acting, thinking and feeling can and should be regarded as behaviors. Behaviorism comprises the position that all theories should have observational correlates but that there are no philosophical differences between publicly observable processes and privately observable processes.
Little Albert	The Little Albert experiment was an experiment showing empirical evidence of classical conditioning in humans. This study was also an example of stimulus generalization. It was conducted in 1920 by John B. Watson along with his assistant Rosalie Rayner.
Backward conditioning	A classical conditioning procedure in which the unconditioned stimulus is presented before the conditioned stimulus is called backward conditioning. It is seldom effective.
Conditioning	Conditioning is a form of associative learning that was first demonstrated by Ivan Pavlov. The typical procedure for inducing classical conditioning involves presentations of a neutral stimulus along with a stimulus of some significance. The neutral stimulus could be any event that does not result in an overt behavioral response from the organism under investigation.
Delayed conditioning	A classical conditioning procedure in which the CS is presented before the US and remains in place until the response occurs is called delayed conditioning.
Simultaneous conditioning	A classical conditioning procedure in which the CS and US are presented at the same time is referred to as simultaneous conditioning.
Stimulus discrimination	The tendency to make a response when stimuli previously associated with reinforcement are present and to withhold the response when not present, is stimulus discrimination.
Stimulus generalization	Stimulus generalization is another learning phenomenon that can be illustrated by CTA. This phenomenon demonstrates that we tend to develop aversions even to types of food that resemble the foods which cause us illness. For example, if one eats an orange and gets sick, one might also avoid eating tangerines and clementines because they look similar to oranges, and might lead one to think that they are also dangerous.
Trace conditioning	A classical conditioning procedure in which the CS is presented and then removed before the US is presented is called trace conditioning.
Higher-order conditioning	In classical conditioning a neutral stimulus comes to elicit a condtioned response(CR) through repeated pairings of the neutral stimulus with a natural or unconditioned stimulus that results in that response. The nuetral stimulus is now called a conditioned stimulus(CS). That CS can also be paired with another nuetral stimulus to produce a higher-order conditioning; a chain of CS-CR relationships.
Spontaneous recovery	Spontaneous recovery is the reemergence of a conditioned response after the conditioning stimulus has been extinguished. It tends to yield somewhat muted responses in which extinction occurs more readily. Spontaneous recovery helps explain why it is so hard to overcome drug addictions.
Law of effect	The law of effect is a principle of psychology described by Edward Thorndike in 1898. It holds that responses to stimuli that produce a satisfying or pleasant effect in a particular situation are more likely to occur again in the situation. Conversely, responses that produce a discomforting or unpleasant effect are less likely to occur again in the situation

Operant conditioning	Operant conditioning is the use of consequences to modify the occurrence and form of behavior. Operant conditioning is distinguished from classical conditioning (also called respondent conditioning, or Pavlovian conditioning) in that Operant conditioning deals with the modification of "voluntary behavior" or operant behavior. Operant behavior "operates" on the environment and is maintained by its consequences, while classical conditioning deals with the conditioning of respondent behaviors which are elicited by antecedent conditions.
Punishment	Punishment is the practice of imposing something unpleasant or aversive on a person or animal in response to an unwanted, disobedient or morally wrong behavior.
Reinforcement	In operant conditioning, reinforcement is an increase in the strength of a response following the change in environment immediately following that response. Response strength can be assessed by measures such as the frequency with which the response is made, or the speed with which it is made.
Primary Reinforcement	The use of reinforcers that are innately or biologically satisfying is called primary reinforcement.
Continuous reinforcement	In continuous reinforcement, every response results in reinforcement.
Intermittent reinforcement	In an intermittent reinforcement schedule, a designated response is reinforced only some of the time.
Partial reinforcement	In a partial reinforcement environment, not every correct response is reinforced. Partial reinforcement is usually introduced after a continuous reinforcement schedule has acquired the behavior.
Schedules of reinforcement	Different combinations of frequency and timing of reinforcement following a behavior are referred to as schedules of reinforcement. They are either continuous (the behavior is reinforced each time it occurs) or intermittent (the behavior is reinforced only on certain occasions).
Negative punishment	Negative punishment occurs when a response decreases as a positive stimulus is removed from the situation.
Positive punishment	In operant conditioning, positive punishment is the presentation of a stimulus after an occurring response decreases the likelihood that the response will be repeated.
Learned helplessness	Learned helplessness is a psychological condition in which a human being or an animal has learned to believe that a situation is helpless. It has come to believe that it has no control over its situation and that whatever it does is futile. As a result, the human being or the animal will stay passive in the face of an unpleasant, harmful or damaging situation, even when it does actually have the power to change its circumstances.
Skinner box	A skinner box is a laboratory apparatus used in the experimental analysis of behavior to study animal behavior. The operant conditioning chamber was created by B. F. Skinner while he was a graduate student at Harvard University around 1930. It is used to study both operant conditioning and classical conditioning.
Active learning	Active learning is an umbrella term that refers to several models of instruction that focus the responsibility of learning on learners. Bonwell and Eison (1991) popularized this approach to instruction. This "buzz word" of the 1980s became their 1990s report to the Association for the Study of Higher Education (ASHE.)

Discrimination	Most broadly, discrimination is the recognition of qualities and differences among certain things or persons and making choices based on those qualities. This article focuses on discrimination amongst people- that is, discrimination based on personal qualities. Discriminating between people on the grounds of merit is generally lawful in Western democracies. Discrimination on other grounds, such as skin color or religion, generally is not. When unlawful discrimination takes place, it is often described as discrimination against a person or group of people.
Cognitive maps	Cognitive maps, mental maps, mind maps, cognitive models code, store, recall, and decode information about the relative locations and attributes of phenomena in their everyday or metaphorical spatial environment.
	The credit of the creation of this term is given to Edward Tolman. Cognitive maps have been studied in various fields, such as psychology, education, archaeology, planning, geography, architecture, landscape architecture , urban planning and management.
Insight	Insight refers to a sudden awareness of the relationships among various elements that had previously appeared to be independent of one another.
Latent learning	The theory of latent learning describes learning that occurs in the absence of an obvious reward. Learning does not depend on reinforcement, but can go on in its absence and show up when reinforcement is introduced. Free exploration can be as effective as many previously reinforced trials according to Tolman.
Scaffolding	Scaffolding is the provision of sufficient supports to promote learning when concepts and skills are being first introduced to students.
Environmental enrichment	Environmental enrichment concerns how the brain is affected by the stimulation of its information processing provided by its surroundings (including the opportunity to interact socially.) Brains in richer, more stimulating environments, have increased numbers of synapses, and the dendrite arbors upon which they reside are more complex. This effect happens particularly during neurodevelopment, but also to a lesser degree in adulthood.
Instinctive drift	The tendency of animals to revert to innate behavior that interferes with learning is called instinctive drift.
Prejudice	The word prejudice refers to prejudgment: i.e. making a decision before becoming aware of the relevant facts of a case. Initially this referred to making a judgment about a person based on their race, before receiving information relevant to the particular issue on which a judgment was being made; it came, however, to be widely used to refer to any hostile attitude towards people based on their race.
Accidental reinforcement	Accidental reinforcement is an unitended behavior that is learned from certain events during a child"s development.
Superstitious behavior	"When small amounts of food are repeatedly given, a 'superstitious ritual' may be set up. This is due not only to the fact that a reinforcing stimulus strengthens any behavior it may happen to follow, even though a contingency has not been explicitly arranged, but also to the fact that the change in behavior resulting from one accidental contingency makes similar accidents more probable."-- Skinner on superstitious behavior.
Encoding	Encoding (in cognition) is a basic perceptual process of interpreting incoming stimuli; technically speaking, it is a complex, multi-stage process of converting relatively objective sensory input (e.g., light, sound) into subjectively meaningful experience.

Encoding	Encoding (in cognition) is a basic perceptual process of interpreting incoming stimuli; technically speaking, it is a complex, multi-stage process of converting relatively objective sensory input (e.g., light, sound) into subjectively meaningful experience.
Storage	The human memory has three processes: encoding (input), Storage and retrieval(output.) Storage is the process of retaining information whether in the sensory memory, the short-term memory or the more permanent long-term memory.
Attention	Attention is the cognitive process of selectively concentrating on one aspect of the environment while ignoring other things. Examples include listening carefully to what someone is saying while ignoring other conversations in the room or listening to a cell phone conversation while driving a car.
Serial-position effect	In what is known as the serial-position effect, items at the beginning of a list are the easiest to recall, followed by the items near the end of a list. Items in the middle are the least likely to be remembered.
Automatic processing	Automatic processing is the processing of information that guides behavior, but without conscious awareness, and without interfering with other conscious activity that may be going on at the same time.
Echoic memory	Echoic memory refers to the phenomenon in which there is a brief mental echo that continues to sound after auditory stimuli has been heard. Echoic memory can be expanded if it is repeated in the phonological loop which rehearses verbal information in order to keep it in short term memory.
Iconic memory	Iconic memory is a type of short term visual memory, named by George Sperling in 1960. Experiments performed by Sperling and colleagues provided evidence for a rapidly decaying sensory trace, lasting for approximately 1000 ms after the offset of a display.
Sensory memory	Sensory memory is the ability to retain impressions of sensory information after the original stimulus has ceased. It refers to items detected by the sensory receptors which are retained temporarily in the sensory registers and which have a large capacity for unprocessed information but are only able to hold accurate images of sensory information momentarily.
Short-term memory	Short-term memory is that part of memory which is said to be able to hold a small amount of information for about 20 seconds. The information held in short-term memory may be: recently processed sensory input; items recently retrieved from long-term memory; or the result of recent mental processing, although that is more generally related to the concept of working memory.
Working memory	Working memory is a theoretical framework within cognitive psychology that refers to the structures and processes used for temporarily storing and manipulating information. There are numerous theories as to both the theoretical structure of working memory as well as to the specific parts of the brain responsible for working memory.
Memory models	Memory models in the C programming language are a way to specify assumptions that the compiler should make when generating code for segmented memory or paged memory platforms.

For example, on the 16-bit x86 platform, six Memory models exist. They control what assumptions are made regarding the segment registers, and the default size of pointers. |

Central executive	The central executive in working memory is, among other things, responsible for directing attention to relevant information, suppressing irrelevant information and inappropriate actions, and for coordinating cognitive processes when more than one task must be done at the same time.
Visual-spatial sketch pad	Visual-spatial sketch pad is assumed to hold information about what we see. It is used in the temporary storage and manipulation of spatial and visual information, such as remembering shapes and colors, or the location or speed of objects in space. It is also involved in tasks which involve planning of spatial movements, like planning one"s way through a complex building.
Declarative memory	Declarative memory is the aspect of human memory that stores facts. It is so called because it refers to memories that can be consciously discussed, or declared. It applies to standard textbook learning and knowledge, as well memories that can be "travelled back to" in one"s "mind"s eye".
Episodic memory	Episodic memory refers to the memory of events, times, places, associated emotions, and other conception-based knowledge in relation to an experience. Semantic and episodic memory together make up the category of declarative memory, which is one of the two major divisions in memory.
Explicit memory	Explicit memory is the conscious, intentional recollection of previous experiences and information.
Procedural memory	Procedural memory is the long-term memory of skills and procedures, or "how to" knowledge.
Semantic memory	Semantic memory refers to the memory of meanings, understandings, and other concept-based knowledge unrelated to specific experiences.
Implicit memory	Implicit memory is a type of memory in which previous experiences aid in the performance of a task without conscious awareness of these previous experiences. Evidence for implicit memory arises in priming, a process whereby subjects show improved performance on tasks for which they have been subconsciously prepared.
Hierarchy	A hierarchy is a system of ranking and organizing things or people, where each element of the system is a subordinate to a single other element.
Priming	Priming in psychology refers to activating parts of particular representations or associations in memory just before carrying out an action or task. It is considered to be one of the manifestations of implicit memory. A property of priming is that the remembered item is remembered best in the form in which it was originally encountered. If a priming list is given in an auditory mode, then an auditory cue produces better performance than a visual cue.
Retrieval cue	Any stimulus or bit of information that aids in the retrieval of particular information from long-term memory is a retrieval cue.
Context-dependent memory	Information that is better retrieved in the context in which it was encoded and stored, or learned is called context-dependent memory.
Mood congruence	In psychiatry, Mood congruence is the congruence between feeling, or the emotion that a person is experiencing, and affect display, or the manner in which that emotion is "presenting", or being expressed.

	In psychology, symptoms are said to be mood-congruent if they are consistent with a patient"s mood or mental disorder. Conversely, they are said to be mood-incongruent if they are inconsistent with their primary mood.
State-dependent memory	State-dependent memory is a phenomenon of learning and recalling that is based upon the physiological and mental state of the organism.
Forgetting	Forgetting is a spontaneous or gradual process in which old memories are unable to be recalled from memory storage. It is subject to delicately balanced optimization that ensures that relevant memories are recalled.
Forgetting curve	Ebbinghaus' forgetting curve illustrates the decline of memory retention in time. A typical graph of the forgetting curve shows that humans tend to halve their memory of newly learned knowledge in a matter of days or weeks unless they consciously review the learned material.
Proactive interference	Proactive interference occurs when information learned earlier disrupts the recall of material learned later. This can become a problem when new information cannot be used correctly as it is interfered with by the older information.
Relearning	Relearning refers to a measure of retention used in experiments on memory. Material is usually relearned more quickly than it is learned initially.
Retroactive interference	Retroactive interference occurs when the material learned later disrupts retrieval of information learned earlier, so old information overlaps with new information.
Cue-dependent forgetting	Cue-dependent forgetting is a failure to recall a memory due to missing associated stimuli or cues that were present at the time the memory was encoded.
Distributed practice	Distributed practice is a technique whereby the student distributes their study efforts in a given course over many study sessions that are relatively short in duration.
Source amnesia	Source amnesia is an explicit memory disorder in which someone can recall certain information, but do not know where or how it was obtained. As source amnesia prohibits recollection of the context specific information surrounding facts in experienced events, there is also the inclusive case of confusion concerning the content or context of events, a highly attributable factor to confabulation in brain disease.
Massed practice	Massed practice refers to learning in one long practice session as opposed to spacing the learning in shorter practice sessions over an extended period.
Misinformation effect	The misinformation effect is a memory bias that occurs when misinformation affects people's reports of their own memory.
Sleeper effect	The sleeper effect identified by psychologist Carl Hovland refers to the "hidden" effect of a propaganda message even when it comes from a discredible source. However, note that the sleeper effect has had something of a checkered history since its original conception.
Primacy effect	The primacy effect is a cognitive bias that results from disproportionate salience of initial stimuli or observations. If, for example, a subject reads a sufficiently-long list of words, he or she is more likely to remember words read toward the beginning than words read in the middle.

Recency effect	Recency effect refers to the tendency to recall the last items in a series of items. The tendency to evaluate others in terms of the most recent impression.
Flashbulb memory	A flashbulb memory is a memory that was laid down in great detail during a personally significant event, often a shocking event of national or international importance.
Long-term potentiation	In neuroscience, long-term potentiation is the long-lasting enhancement in communication between two neurons that results from stimulating them simultaneously.
Hippocampus	The hippocampus is a part of the brain located in the medial temporal lobe. It forms a part of the limbic system and plays a part in memory and spatial navigation.
Engram	An engram is a hypothetical means by which memories are stored as physical or biochemical change in the brain in response to external stimuli.
Amnesia	Amnesia is a condition in which memory is disturbed. The causes of amnesia are organic or functional. Organic causes include damage to the brain, through trauma or disease, or use of certain generally sedative drugs.
Anterograde amnesia	Anterograde amnesia is a form of amnesia, or memory loss; in which new events are not transferred from short-termed memory to long-term memory. This may be a permanent deficit, or it may be temporary, such as is sometimes seen for a period of hours or days after head trauma or for a period of intoxication with an amnestic drug.
Retrograde amnesia	Retrograde amnesia is a form of amnesia where someone will be unable to recall events that occurred before the onset of amnesia. The term is used to categorise patterns of symptoms, rather than to indicate a particular cause or etiology.
Criminal justice	Criminal justice is the system of, practices, and organizations, used by national and local governments, directed at maintaining social control, deter and controlling crime, and sanctioning those who violate laws with criminal penalties. The pursuit of criminal justice is, like all forms of "justice," "fairness" or "process," essentially the pursuit of an ideal.
Overlearning	Continued rehearsal of material after one first appears to have mastered it is called overlearning.
Time management	Time management refers to a range of skills, tools, and techniques used to manage time when accomplishing specific tasks, projects and goals. This set encompass a wide scope of activities, and these include planning, allocating, setting goals, delegation, analysis of time spent, monitoring, organizing, scheduling, and prioritizing. Initially Time management referred to just business or work activities, but eventually the term broadened to include personal activities also.
Mnemonic	A mnemonic is an aid for memory . They rely not only on repetition to remember facts, but also on associations between easy-to-remember constructs and lists of data, based on the principle that the human mind much more easily remembers insignificant data attached to spatial, personal, or otherwise meaningful information than that occurring in meaningless sequences.

Cognition	In psychology, cognition refers to an information processing view of an individual"s psychological functions. Other interpretations of the meaning of cognition link it to the development of concepts; individual minds, groups, organizations, and even larger coalitions of entities, can be modelled as societies which cooperate to form concepts.
Concepts	There are two prevailing theories in contemporary philosophy which attempt to explain the nature of Concepts The representational theory of mind proposes that Concepts are mental representations, while the semantic theory of Concepts (originating with Frege"s distinction between concept and object) holds that they are abstract objects. Ideas are taken to be Concepts, although abstract Concepts do not necessarily appear to the mind as images as some ideas do.
Problem solving	Problem solving forms part of thinking. Considered the most complex of all intellectual functions, problem solving has been defined as higher-order cognitive process that requires the modulation and control of more routine or fundamental skills.
Creativity	Creativity is a mental process involving the generation of new ideas or concepts, or new associations between existing ideas or concepts.
Language	A Language is a system for encoding and decoding information. In its most common use, the term refers to so-called "natural Language s" -- the forms of communication considered peculiar to humankind. In linguistics the term is extended to refer to the human cognitive facility of creating and using Language
Linguistic relativity hypothesis	The linguistic relativity hypothesis states that there is a systematic relationship between the grammatical categories of the language a person speaks and how that person both understands the world and behaves in it.
Grammar	Grammar is the study of the rules governing the use of a given natural language, and, as such, is a field of linguistics. Traditionally, grammar included morphology and syntax; in modern linguistics these subfields are complemented by phonetics, phonology, orthography, semantics, and pragmatics.
Semantics	Semantics refers to aspects of meaning, as expressed in language or other systems of signs.
Syntax	In linguistics, syntax are the rules of a language that show how the words of that language are to be arranged to make a sentence of that language. The term syntax can also be used to refer to these rules themselves, as in "the syntax of Gaelic". Modern research in syntax attempts to describe languages in terms of such rules, and, for many practitioners, to find general rules that apply to all languages. Since the field of syntax attempts to explain grammatical judgments, and not provide them, it is unconcerned with linguistic prescription.
Language development	Language development is a process that starts early in human life, when a person begins to acquire language by learning it as it is spoken and by mimicry. Children"s language development moves from simplicity to complexity. Infants start without language. Yet by four months of age, babies can read lips and discriminate speech sounds.
Babbling	Babbling is a stage in child language acquisition, during which an infant appears to be experimenting with uttering sounds of language, but not yet producing any recognizable words.
Cooing	Cooing is the spontaneous repetition of vowel sounds by infants.

Telegraphic speech	Telegraphic speech, according to linguistics and psychology, is speech during the two-word stage of language acquisition in children, which is laconic and efficient.
Intelligence	Intelligence is a property of mind that encompasses many related abilities, such as the capacities to reason, plan, solve problems, think abstractly, comprehend ideas and language, and learn. In some cases intelligence may include traits such as creativity, personality, character, knowledge, or wisdom. However other psychologists prefer not to include these traits in the definition of intelligence.
Crystallized intelligence	In psychometric psychology, fluid and crystallized intelligence are factors of general intelligence identified by Raymond Cattell. The terms are somewhat misleading because one is not a "crystallized" form of the other. Rather, they are believed to be separate neural and mental systems.
Multiple intelligences	Multiple intelligences is educational theory put forth by psychologist Howard Gardner, which suggests that an array of different kinds of "intelligence" exists in human beings. He suggests that each individual manifests varying levels of these different intelligences, and thus each person has a unique "cognitive profile."
Theory of multiple intelligences	Theory of multiple intelligences is educational theory put forth by psychologist Howard Gardner, which suggests that an array of different kinds of "intelligence" exists in human beings. The theory was proposed in the context of debates about the concept of intelligence, and whether methods which claim to measure intelligence are truly scientific.
Analytical intelligence	Analytical intelligence involves the ability to analyze, judge, evaluate, compare, and contrast.
Practical intelligence	Practical intelligence focuses on the ability to use, apply, implement, and put into practice.
Wechsler Adult Intelligence Scale	Wechsler Adult Intelligence Scale is a general test of intelligence IQ, published in February 1955 as a revision of the Wechsler-Bellevue test 1939, a battery of tests that is composed from subtests Wechsler "adopted" from the Army Tests. Weschler defined intelligence as "The global capacity of a person to act purposefully, to think rationally, and to deal effectively with his/her environment."
Wechsler Intelligence Scale for Children	The Wechsler Intelligence Scale for Children, developed by David Wechsler, is an intelligence test for children between the ages of 6 and 16 inclusive that can be completed without reading or writing. The WISC generates an IQ score.
Wechsler Preschool and Primary Scale of Intelligence	The Wechsler Preschool and Primary Scale of Intelligence is an intelligence test designed for children ages 2 years 6 months to 7 years 3 months developed by David Wechsler in 1967. It is a descendent of the earlier Wechsler Adult Intelligence Scale and the Wechsler Intelligence Scale for Children tests. It has since been revised twice, in 1989 and 2002.
Mental retardation	Mental retardation is a term for a pattern of persistently slow learning of basic motor and language skills during childhood, and a significantly below-normal global intellectual capacity as an adult. One common criterion for diagnosis of mental retardation is a tested intelligence quotient of 70 or below and deficits in adaptive functioning. People with mental retardation may be described as having developmental disabilities, global developmental delay, or learning difficulties.

Down syndrome	Down syndrome or is a genetic disorder caused by the presence of all or part of an extra 21st chromosome. Often Down syndrome is associated with some impairment of cognitive ability and physical growth as well as facial appearance. Down syndrome can be identified during pregnancy or at birth.
Phenylketonuria	Phenylketonuria is an autosomal recessive genetic disorder characterized by a deficiency in the enzyme phenylalanine hydroxylase. This enzyme is necessary to metabolize the amino acid phenylalanine to the amino acid tyrosine. When PAH is deficient, phenylalanine accumulates and is converted into phenylketones, which are detected in the urine.
Savant syndrome	Savant syndrome describes a person having both a severe developmental or mental handicap but with extraordinary mental abilities not found in most people. This means a lower than average general intelligence ut very high narrow intelligence in one or more fields. Savant Syndrome skills involve striking feats of memory and arithmetic calculation and sometimes include unusual abilities in art or music.
Symbolic interactionism	Symbolic interactionism is a major sociological perspective that is influential in many areas of the discipline. It is particularly important in microsociology and social psychology. Symbolic interactionism is derived from American pragmatism and particularly from the work of George Herbert Mead, who argued that people"s selves are social products, but that these selves are also purposive and creative.
Maturation	Maturation is the process of becoming mature. The emergence of personal and behavioral characteristics through growth processes. The final stages of differentiation of cells, tissues, or organs
Cohort effect	The term cohort effect is used in social science to describe variations in the characteristics of an area of study over time among individuals who are defined by some shared temporal experience or common life experience, such as year of birth, or year of exposure to radiation.
Cross-sectional study	A Cross-sectional study forms a class of research methods that involve observation of some subset of a population of items all at the same time, in which, groups can be compared at different ages with respect of independent variables, such as, IQ, memory. It can be thought of as providing a "snapshot" of the frequency and characteristics of a disease in a population at a particular point in time.
Generalizability	Generalizability is a statistical framework for conceptualizing, investigating, and designing reliable observations. It was originally introduced by Lee Cronbach and his colleagues. It is suitable in the context of highly controlled laboratory conditions, variance is a part of everyday life. In field research, for example, it is unrealistic to expect that the conditions of measurement will remain constant.
Longitudinal research	Research that studies the same subjects over an extended period of time, usually several years or more, is called longitudinal research.
Fertilization	Fertilization is fusion of gametes to form a new organism of the same species. In animals, the process involves a sperm fusing with an ovum, which eventually leads to the development of an embryo.
Drug abuse	Drug abuse has a wide range of definitions related to taking a psychoactive drug or performance enhancing drug for a non-therapeutic or non-medical effect.

Placenta	The Placenta is an organ unique to mammals that connects the developing fetus to the uterine wall. The Placenta supplies the fetus with oxygen and food, and allows fetal waste to be disposed of via the maternal kidneys. The word Placenta comes from the Latin for cake, from Greek plakóenta/plakoúnta, accusative of plakóeis/plakoús - πλακΐŒεις, πλακοΐ□ς, "flat, slab-like", referring to its round, flat appearance in humans.
Placental barrier	The placental barrier between the fetus and the wall of the mother's uterus allows for the transfer of materials from mother, and eliminates waste products of fetus.
Fetal alcohol syndrome	Fetal alcohol syndrome is a disorder of permanent birth defects that occurs in the offspring of women who drink alcohol during pregnancy. Alcohol crosses the placental barrier and can stunt fetal growth or weight, create distinctive facial stigmata, damage neurons and brain structures, and cause other physical, mental, or behavioral problems.
Prosencephalon	In the anatomy of the brain of vertebrates, the prosencephalon is the rostral-most portion of the brain. The prosencephalon, the mesencephalon, and rhombencephalon are the three primary portions of the brain during early development of the central nervous system.
Hindbrain	The hindbrain is a developmental categorization of portions of the central nervous system in vertebrates. It can be subdivided in a variable number of transversal swellings called rhombomeres.
Midbrain	The midbrain is the middle of three vesicles that arise from the neural tube that forms the brain of developing animals. In mature human brains, it becomes the least differentiated, from both its developmental form and within its own structure, among the three vesicles. The midbrain is considered part of the brain stem.
Reflex	A reflex action is an automatic neuromuscular action elicited by a defined stimulus. In most contexts, especially involving humans, a reflex action is mediated via the reflex arc
Myelin	Myelin is an electrically-insulating phospholipid layer that surrounds the axons of many neurons. It is an outgrowth of glial cells: Schwann cells supply the myelin for peripheral neurons, whereas oligodendrocytes supply it to those of the central nervous system.
Synaptic pruning	Synaptic pruning is a neurological regulatory process, which facilitates a productive change in neural structure by reducing the overall number of overproduced or "weak" neurons into more efficient synaptic configurations. It is often a synonym used to describe the maturation of behavior and cognitive intelligence in children by "weeding out" the weaker synapses.
Puberty	Puberty refers to the process of physical changes by which a child"s body becomes an adult body capable of reproduction.
Adolescence	Adolescence is a transitional stage of human development that occurs toward the end of childhood and the beginning of adulthood.
Menarche	Menarche is the first menstrual period, or first menstrual bleeding in the females of human beings. From both social and medical perspectives it is often considered the central event of female puberty, as it signals the possibility of fertility. Timing of menarche is influenced by both genetic and environmental factors, especially nutritional status.

Menopause	The word menopause literally means the permanent physiological, or natural, cessation of menstrual cycles. In other words, menopause means the natural and permanent stopping of the monthly female reproductive cycles, and in humans this is usually indicated by a permanent absence of monthly periods or menstruation.
Secondary sex characteristics	Secondary sex characteristics are traits that distinguish the two sexes of a species, but that are not directly part of the reproductive system. They are believed to have evolved to give an individual an advantage over its rivals in courtship. They are opposed to the primary sexual characteristics: the sex organs.
Spermarche	The first ejaculatory experience of boys is termed spermarche. It contrasts with menarche in girls. Depending on their upbringing, cultural differences, and prior sexual knowledge, boys may have different reactions to spermarche, ranging from fear to excitement.
Middle age	Middle age is the period of life beyond young adulthood but before the onset of old age.
Male	Male (♂,) refers to the sex of an organism which produces small mobile gametes, called spermatozoa. Each spermatozoon can fuse with a larger fe Male gamete or ovum, in the process of fertilization. A Male cannot reproduce sexually without access to at least one ovum from a fe Male , but some organisms can reproduce both sexually and asexually.
Late adulthood	The developmental period that lasts from about 60 to 70 years of age until death is referred to as late adulthood.
Hayflick limit	The Hayflick limit was the observation that cells dividing in cell culture divided about 50 times before dying. As cells approach this limit, they show more signs of old age.
Cognitive development	Cognitive development concerns the emergence and acquisition of schemata schemes of how one perceives the world in "developmental stages", times when children are acquiring new ways of mentally representing information.
Accommodation	Accommodation can be understood as the mechanism by which failure leads to learning: when we act on the expectation that the world operates in one way and it violates our expectations, we often fail, but by accommodation of this new experience and reframing our model of the way the world works, we learn from the experience of failure, or others" failure.
Object permanence	Object permanence is the term used to describe the awareness that objects continue to exist even when they are no longer visible. Jean Piaget conducted experiments with infants which led him to conclude that this awareness was typically achieved at eight to nine months of age, during the sensorimotor stage of cognitive development. He concluded that some infants were too young to understand object permanence, which would tend to explain why they did not cry when their mothers were gone.
Preoperational stage	The Preoperational stage is the second of four stages of cognitive development. By observing sequences of play, Piaget was able to demonstrate that towards the end of the second year a qualitatively new kind of psychological functioning occurs.
Sensorimotor period	Infants are born with a set of congenital reflexes, according to Piaget, in addition to a drive to explore their world. Their initial schemas are formed through differentiation of the congenital reflexes. The sensorimotor period is the first of the four periods.

Stages	Stages represent relatively discrete periods of time in which functioning is qualitatively different from functioning at other periods.
Adolescent egocentrism	The quality of thinking that leads some adolescents to believe that they are the focus of attention in social situations, to believe that their problems are unique, to be unusually hypocritical, and to be pseudostupid is adolescent egocentrism.
Self-consciousness	Self-consciousness is an acute sense of self-awareness. It is a preoccupation with oneself, rather than the philosophical state of self-awareness, which is the awareness that one exists as an individual being.
Personal fable	The personal fable is term coined by David Elkind that is used in psychology to describe a form of egocentrism normally exhibited during early adolescence, and it is characterized by an over-differentiating of one"s experiences and feelings from others to the point of assuming those experiences are unique from those of others.
Imaginary audience	The imaginary audience refers to an egocentric state where an individual imagines and believes that multitudes of people are enthusiastically listening to him or her at all times. Though this state is often exhibited in young adolescence, people of any age may harbor a belief in an imaginary audience.
Contact comfort	A hypothethetical primary drive to seek physical comfort through contact with another is called contact comfort.
Imprinting	Imprinting is the term used in psychology and ethology to describe any kind of phase-sensitive learning that is rapid and apparently independent of the consequences of behavior. It was first used to describe situations in which an animal or person learns the characteristics of some stimulus, which is therefore said to be "imprinted" onto the subject.
Romantic love	An intense, positive emotion that involves sexual attraction, feelings of caring, and the belief that one is in love is romantic love.
Moral development	Moral development is a field of psychology studying the development regarding rules and conventions about what people should do in their interactions with other people.
Moral reasoning	Moral reasoning is a study in psychology that overlaps with moral philosophy. The term is sometimes used in a different sense: reasoning under conditions of uncertainty, such as obtain in a court of law. It is this sense that gave rise to the phrase, "To a moral certainty;" however, this sense is now little used outside of charges to juries.
Post-conventional level	The post-conventional level consists of stages five and six of moral development. Realization that individuals are separate entities from society now becomes salient. One"s own perspective should be viewed before the society"s. It is due to this "nature of self before others" that the post-conventional level is sometimes mistaken for pre-conventional behaviors.
Temperament	In psychology, temperament is the innate aspect of an individual"s personality, such as introversion or extroversion.Temperament is defined as that part of the personality which is genetically based. Along with character, and those aspects acquired through learning, the two together are said to constitute personality.
Ego integrity versus despair	Ego integrity versus despair is a term coined by Erik Erikson regarding the crisis of late adulthood, characterized by the task of maintaining one"s sense of identity despite physical deterioration.

Divorce	Divorce is the ending of a marriage before the death of either spouse.
Domestic violence	Domestic violence occurs when a family member, partner or ex-partner attempts to physically or psychologically dominate another. Domestic violence often refers to violence between spouses, but can also include cohabitants and non-married intimate partners.
Disengagement theory	Disengagement theory delineates how relationships between people and other members of society are severed or altered in quality; each of these events constitute a form of disengagement.
Thanatology	Thanatology is the academic, and often scientific, study of death among human beings. It investigates the circumstances surrounding a person"s death, the grief experienced by the deceased"s loved ones, and larger social attitudes towards death such as ritual and memorialization. It is primarily an interdisciplinary study, frequently undertaken by professionals in nursing, psychology, sociology, psychiatry, and social work.
Social learning theory	Social learning theory is a theory to explain how people learn behavior. People learn through observing others" behavior. If people observe positive, desired outcomes in the observed behavior, they are more likely to model, imitate, and adopt the behavior themselves.
Cloacal exstrophy	Cloacal exstrophy is a severe birth defect wherein much of the abdominal organs are exposed. It often causes the splitting of both male and female genitalia, and the anus is occasionally sealed.
Sexual orientation	Sexual orientation refers to the direction of an individual"s sexuality, usually conceived of as classifiable according to the sex or gender of the persons whom the individual finds sexually attractive. Most definitions of sexual orientation include a psychological component and/or a behavioral component.
Transsexualism	Transsexualism is a condition in which a person identifies with a physical sex different from the one that they were born with or assigned in cases where ambiguity of the child"s sex organs led to assigning them a physical sex.
Bisexuality	Bisexuality is a sexual orientation which refers to the romantic and/or sexual attraction of individuals to other individuals of both their own and the opposite gender or sex. Bisexuality is often misunderstood as a form of adultery or polyamory, and a popular misconception is that bisexuals must always be in relationships with men and women simultaneously.
Androgyny	Androgyny refers to two concepts regarding the mixing of both male and female genders or having a lack of gender identification. The first is the mixing of masculine and feminine characteristics and second is in describing something that is neither masculine nor feminine. Physiological androgyny, which deals with physical traits, is distinct from behavioral androgyny which deals with personal and social anomalies in gender, and from psychological androgyny, which is a matter of gender identity.
Experiment	In the scientific method, an experiment is a set of observations performed in the context of solving a particular problem or question, to support or falsify a hypothesis or research concerning phenomena. The experiment is a cornerstone in the empirical approach to acquiring deeper knowledge about the physical world.
Ethnocentrism	Ethnocentrism is the tendency to look at the world primarily from the perspective of one's own culture.

Masters and Johnson	Masters and Johnson produced the four stage model of sexual response, which they described as the human sexual response cycle. They defined the four stages of this cycle as: excitement phase, plateau phase, orgasm, and resolution phase.
Sexual behavior	Human Sexual behavior refers to the manner in which humans experience and express their sexuality. It encompass a wide range of activities such as strategies to find or attract partners (mating and display behaviour), interactions between individuals, physical or emotional intimacy, and sexual contact. Although some cultures hold that sexual activity is acceptable only within marriage, extramarital sexual activities still takes place within such cultures.
Ejaculation	Ejaculation is the ejecting of semen from the penis, and is usually accompanied by orgasm. It is usually the result of sexual stimulation, which may include prostate stimulation. Rarely, it is due to prostatic disease. Ejaculation may occur spontaneously during sleep a nocturnal emission.
Partible paternity	Partible paternity is where the nurture of a child is shared by multiple fathers, a form of polyandry. This may be, and probably has been, read as the women of the tribe being the communal property of the males.
Same-sex marriage	Same-sex marriage is a term for a governmentally, socially, or religiously recognized marriage in which two people of the same sex live together as a family.
Homophobia	An intense, irrational hostility toward or fear of homosexuals is referred to as homophobia.
Dyspareunia	Dyspareunia is painful sexual intercourse, due to medical or psychological causes. The term is used almost exclusively in women, although the problem can also occur in men. The causes are often reversible, even when long-standing, but self-perpetuating pain is a factor after the original cause has been removed.
Erectile dysfunction	Erectile dysfunction is a sexual dysfunction characterized by the inability to develop or maintain an erection of the penis. There are various underlying causes, such as cardiovascular leakage and diabetes, many of which are medically treatable.
Premature ejaculation	Premature ejaculation is the most common sexual problem in men, characterized by a lack of voluntary control over ejaculation
Vaginismus	Vaginismus is a condition where the muscles at the entrance to vagina contract, preventing successful sexual intercourse. It is most commonly caused by a psychological reaction but it may sometimes be due to vaginal inflammation or damage.
Sex therapy	Sex therapy is the treatment of sexual dysfunction, such as non-consumation, premature ejaculation or erectile dysfunction, problems commonly caused by stress, tiredness and other environmental and relationship factors.
Viagra	Sildenafil citrate, sold as Viagra Revatio and under various other trade names, is a drug used to treat erectile dysfunction and pulmonary arterial hypertension (PAH.) It was developed and is being marketed by the pharmaceutical company Pfizer. It acts by inhibiting cGMP specific phosphodiesterase type 5, an enzyme that regulates blood flow in the penis.

Cybersex	Cybersex is a virtual sex encounter in which two or more persons connected remotely via a computer network send one another sexually explicit messages describing a sexual experience. It is a form of role-playing in which the participants pretend they are having actual sexual relations. In one iteration, this fantasy sex is accomplished by the participants describing their actions and responding to their chat partners in a mostly written form designed to stimulate their own sexual feelings and fantasies. Cybersex may also be accomplished through the use of avatars in a multiuser software environment.
Acquired immune deficiency syndrome	Acquired immune deficiency syndrome is a collection of symptoms and infections resulting from the specific damage to the immune system caused by the human immunodeficiency virus in humans, and similar viruses in other species.
Safe sex	Safe sex is the practice of sexual activity in a manner that reduces the risk of infection with sexually transmitted diseases Conversely, un Safe sex is the practice of sexual intercourse or other sexual contact without regard for prevention of STDs.
Homeostasis	Homeostasis is the property of either an open system or a closed system, especially a living organism, which regulates its internal environment so as to maintain a stable, constant condition.
Regression	Regression toward the mean, in statistics, is the phenomenon whereby members of a population with extreme values on a given measure for one observation will, for purely statistical reasons, probably give less extreme measurements on other occasions when they are observed.
Sensation seeking	A generalized preference for high or low levels of sensory stimulation is referred to as sensation seeking.
Test anxiety	High levels of arousal and worry that seriously impair test performance is referred to as test anxiety.
Lateral hypothalamus	The Lateral hypothalamus is a part of the hypothalamus. The Lateral hypothalamus is concerned with hunger. Any damage sustained to the lateral hypothalamus can cause reduced food intake.
Ventromedial hypothalamus	Ventromedial hypothalamus acts as a satiety center and, when activated, signals an animal to stop eating; when destroyed, the animal overeats, becoming obese.
Obesity	Obesity is a condition in which excess body fat has accumulated to an extent that health may be negatively affected. It is commonly defined as a body mass index (BMI) of 30 kg/m^2 or higher. This distinguishes it from being pre-obese or overweight as defined by a BMI of 25 kg/m^2 but less than 30 kg/m^2.
Anorexia nervosa	Anorexia nervosa is a psychiatric diagnosis that describes an eating disorder characterized by low body weight and body image distortion with an obsessive fear of gaining weight. Anorexia Nervosa is a disease condition that can put a serious strain on many of the body"s organs and physiological resources.
Bulimia nervosa	Bulimia nervosa is an eating disorder. It is a psychological condition in which the subject engages in recurrent binge eating followed by intentional purging. This purging is done in order to compensate for the excessive intake of food, usually to prevent weight gain. It is often less about food, more to do with deep psychological issues and profound feelings of lack of control.
Achievement motivation	The psychological need in humans for success is called achievement motivation.

Behavioral genetics	Behavioral genetics is the field of biology that studies the role of genetics in animal behavior.
Need for achievement	Need for Achievement refers to an individual"s desire for significant accomplishment, mastering of skills, control, or high standards. The term was introduced by the psychologist, David McClelland. Need for Achievement is related to the difficulty of tasks people choose to undertake.
Thematic Apperception Test	Thematic Apperception Test has been amongst the most widely used, researched, and taught projective psychological tests. Its adherents claim that it taps a subject"s unconscious to reveal repressed aspects of personality, motives and needs for achievement, power and intimacy, and problem-solving abilities.
Limbic system	The limbic system includes the putative structures in the human brain involved in emotion, motivation, and emotional association with memory. The limbic system influences the formation of memory by integrating emotional states with stored memories of physical sensations.
Parasympathetic nervous system	The parasympathetic nervous system is a division of the autonomic nervous system, along with the sympathetic nervous system and Enteric nervous system. The ANS is a subdivision of the peripheral nervous system.
Sympathetic nervous system	The Sympathetic nervous system is a branch of the autonomic nervous system. It is always active at a basal level and becomes more active during times of stress. Its actions during the stress response comprise the fight-or-flight response. The sympathetic nervous system is responsible for up- and down-regulating many homeostatic mechanisms in living organisms.
Facial-feedback hypothesis	The view that stereotypical facial expressions can contribute to stereotypical emotions is called the facial-feedback hypothesis.
Subliminal perception	Subliminal perception is a signal or message embedded in another object, designed to pass below the normal limits of perception. These messages are indiscernible by the conscious mind, but allegedly affect the subconscious or deeper mind.
Extrinsic motivation	Responding to external incentives such as rewards and punishments is form of extrinsic motivation. Traditionally, extrinsic motivation has been used to motivate employees: Payments, rewards, control, or punishments.
Intrinsic motivation	Intrinsic motivation causes people to engage in an activity for its own sake. They are subjective factors and include self-determination, curiosity, challenge, effort, and others.
Emotional intelligence	The expression emotional intelligence indicates a kind of intelligence or skill that involves the ability to perceive, assess and positively influence one"s own and other people"s emotions.
Polygraph	A polygraph is a device which measures and records several physiological variables such as blood pressure, heart rate, respiration and skin conductivity while a series of questions is being asked, in an attempt to detect lies.

Factor analysis	Factor analysis is a statistical technique that originated in psychometrics. The objective is to explain the most of the variability among a number of observable random variables in terms of a smaller number of unobservable random variables called factors.
Defense mechanisms	In Freudian psychoanalytic theory, Defense mechanisms are psychological strategies brought into play by various entities to cope with reality and to maintain self-image. Healthy persons normally use different defences throughout life. An ego defence mechanism becomes pathological only when its persistent use leads to maladaptive behavior such that the physical and/or mental health of the individual is adversely affected.
Morality	Morality has three principal meanings. In its first descriptive usage, morality means a code of conduct held to be authoritative in matters of right and wrong, whether by society, philosophy, religion, or individual conscience. Roberts, Jr. has offered a perspective in which morality, and specifically the capacity for guilt, is viewed as a maladaptive byproduct of the evolution of rationality.
Rationalization	Rationalization is the process of constructing a logical justification for a decision that was originally arrived at through a different mental process. It is one of Freud's defense mechanisms.
Reality principle	The reality principle tells us to subordinate pleasure to what needs to be done. Subordinating the pleasure principle to the reality principle is done through a psychological process Freud calls sublimation, where you take desires that can't be fulfilled, or shouldn't be fulfilled, and turn their energy into something useful and productive.
Super-ego	The super-ego tends to stand in opposition to the desires of the id because of their conflicting objectives, and is aggressive towards the ego. The super-ego acts as the conscience, maintaining our sense of morality and the prohibition of taboos.
Pleasure principle	The pleasure principle is the tendency to seek pleasure and avoid pain. In Freud"s theory, this principle rules the Id, but is at least partly repressed by the reality principle.
Displacement	In psychology, displacement is a subconscious defense mechanism whereby the mind redirects affects from an object felt to be dangerous or unacceptable to an object felt to be safe or acceptable.
Intellectualization	Intellectualization is a defense mechanism where reasoning is used to block confrontation with an unconscious conflict and its associated emotional stress.
Projection	Attributing one's own undesirable thoughts, impulses, traits, or behaviors to others is referred to as projection.
Reaction formation	In Freud's psychoanalytic theory, reaction formation is a defense mechanism in which anxiety-producing or unacceptable emotions are replaced by their direct opposites.
Regression	Regression toward the mean, in statistics, is the phenomenon whereby members of a population with extreme values on a given measure for one observation will, for purely statistical reasons, probably give less extreme measurements on other occasions when they are observed.
Repression	A defense mechanism, repression involves moving thoughts unacceptable to the ego into the unconscious, where they cannot be easily accessed.

Sublimation	Sublimation is a coping mechanism. It refers to rechanneling sexual or aggressive energy into pursuits that society considers acceptable or admirable.
Psychosexual stages	In Freudian theory each child passes through five psychosexual stages. During each stage, the id focuses on a distinct erogenous zone on the body. Suffering from trauma during any of the first three stages may result in fixation in that stage. Freud related the resolutions of the stages with adult personalities and personality disorders.
Anal-expulsive personality	A disorderly, destructive, cruel, or messy person has by psychoanalytic terms an anal-expulsive personality.
Oedipus complex	The Oedipus complex in Freudian psychoanalysis refers to a stage of psychosexual development in childhood where children of both sexes regard their father as an adversary and competitor for the exclusive love of their mother. The name derives from the Greek myth of Oedipus, who unknowingly kills his father, Laius, and marries his mother, Jocasta.
Penis envy	Penis envy in Freudian psychoanalysis refers to the theorized reaction of a girl during her psychosexual development to the realisation that she does not have a penis. Freud considered this realisation a defining moment in the development of gender and sexual identity for women.
Analytical psychology	Analytical psychology is the school of psychology originating from the ideas of Swiss psychiatrist Carl Jung, and then advanced by his students and other thinkers who followed in his tradition. It is distinct from Freudian psychoanalysis but also has a number of similarities. Its aim is the apprehension and integration of the deep forces and motivations underlying human behavior by the practice of an accumulative phenomenology around the significance of dreams, folklore and mythology.
Archetypes	Archetypes are, according to Swiss psychiatrist Carl Jung, innate universal psychic dispositions that form the substrate from which the basic themes of human life emerge. Being universal and innate, their influence can be detected in the form of myths, symbols, rituals and instincts of human beings. Archetypes are components of the collective unconscious and serve to organize, direct and inform human thought and behaviour.
Collective unconscious	Collective unconscious is a term of analytical psychology originally coined by Carl Jung. Jung distinguished the collective unconscious from the personal unconscious particular to each human being.
Infantile sexuality	Freud's insistence that sexuality does not begin with adolescence, that babies are sexual too, is referred to as infantile sexuality.
Inferiority complex	An inferiority complex, in the fields of psychology and psychoanalysis, is a feeling that one is inferior to others in some way.
Anima and animus	In Carl Jung"s school of analytical psychology, anima and animus refer to the unconscious or true inner self of an individual, as opposed to the persona, or outer aspect of the personality; and the feminine inner personality, as present in the unconscious of the male. It is in contrast to the animus, which represents masculine characteristics in the female. It can be identified as all of the unconscious feminine psychological qualities that a male possesses.
Basic anxiety	Basic anxiety is a child's insecurity and doubt when a parent is indifferent, unloving, or disparaging. This anxiety, according to Horney, leads the child to a basic hostility toward his or her parents. The child may then become neurotic as an adult.

Self-concept	Self-concept is the mental and conceptual understanding and persistent regard that sentient beings hold for their own existence. Components of the self-concept include physical, psychological, and social attributes, which can be influenced by the individual"s attitudes, habits, beliefs and ideas. These components and attributes can not be condensed to the general concepts of self-image and the self-esteem.
Unconditional positive regard	Unqualified caring and nonjudgmental acceptance of another is called unconditional positive regard.
Self-actualization	Self-actualization is the instinctual need of humans to make the most of their abilities and to strive to be the best they can. It is the intrinsic growth of what is already in the organism, or more accurately, of what the organism is.
Reciprocal determinism	Reciprocal determinism is the theory set forth by psychologist Albert Bandura that a person"s behavior both influences and is influenced by personal factors and the social environment. Bandura accepts the possibility of an individual"s behavior being conditioned through the use of consequences. At the same time he asserts that a person"s behavior can impact the environment.
Self-efficacy	Self-efficacy is an impression that one is capable of performing in a certain manner or attaining certain goals. It is a belief that one has the capabilities to execute the courses of actions required to manage prospective situations. Self esteem relates to a person's sense of self-worth, whereas self-efficacy relates to a person's perception of their ability to reach a goal.
Minnesota Multiphasic Personality Inventory	The Minnesota Multiphasic Personality Inventory is one of the most frequently used personality tests in mental health. The test is used by trained professionals to assist in identifying personality structure and psychopathology. The original authors of the Minnesota Multiphasic Personality Inventory were Starke R. Hathaway, PhD, and J. C. McKinley, MD.
Rorschach Inkblot Test	The Rorschach inkblot test is a method of psychological evaluation. Psychologists use this test to try to examine the personality characteristics and emotional functioning of their patients. The Rorschach is currently the second most commonly used test in forensic assessment, after the MMPI, and is the second most widely used test by members of the Society for Personality Assessment. It has been employed in diagnosing underlying thought disorder and differentiating psychotic from nonpsychotic thinking in cases where the patient is reluctant to openly admit to psychotic thinking.
Thematic Apperception Test	Thematic Apperception Test has been amongst the most widely used, researched, and taught projective psychological tests. Its adherents claim that it taps a subject"s unconscious to reveal repressed aspects of personality, motives and needs for achievement, power and intimacy, and problem-solving abilities.
Fallacy of positive instances	The tendency to remember or notice information that fits one's expectations, while forgetting discrepancies, is referred to as the fallacy of positive instances.
Self-serving bias	A self-serving bias is the tendency to view one"s successes as stemming from internal factors and one"s failures as stemming from external factors.
Ethnocentrism	Ethnocentrism is the tendency to look at the world primarily from the perspective of one's own culture.
Culture-bound disorders	Abnormal syndromes found only in a few cultural groups are called culture-bound disorders.

85

Somatization	Somatization is currently defined as "a tendency to experience and communicate somatic distress in response to psychosocial stress and to seek medical help for it".
Asylums	Asylums are hospitals specializing in the treatment of persons with mental illness. Psychiatric wards differ only in that they are a unit of a larger hospital.
Exorcism	Exorcism is the practice of evicting demons or other spiritual entities from a person or place which they are believed to have possessed. The practice is quite ancient and part of the belief system of many countries.
	In Christian practice the person performing the Exorcism known as an exorcist, is often a member of the church, or an individual thought to be graced with special powers or skills.
Trephining	Trephining is a form of surgery in which a hole is drilled or scraped into the skull, leaving the membrane around the brain intact. It addresses health problems that relate to abnormal intracranial pressure.
Diagnostic and Statistical Manual of Mental Disorders	The Diagnostic and Statistical Manual of Mental Disorders is a handbook for mental health professionals that lists different categories of mental disorder and the criteria for diagnosing them, according to the publishing organization the American Psychiatric Association.
Insanity	Insanity is the behavior whereby a person flouts societal norms and becomes a danger to himself and others. Psychologically, it is a general popular and legal term defining behavior influenced by mental instability. Today it is most commonly encountered as an informal term or in the narrow legal context of the insanity defense, and in the medical profession the term is now avoided in favour of specific diagnoses of mental illness as schizophrenia and other psychotic disorders.
Delirium	Delirium is a medical term used to describe an acute decline in attention and cognition. Delirium is probably the single most common acute disorder affecting adults in general hospitals. It affects 10-20% of all adults in hospital, and 30-40% of older patients.
Dementia	Dementia is the progressive decline in cognitive function due to damage or disease in the brain beyond what might be expected from normal aging.
Generalized anxiety disorder	Generalized anxiety disorder is an anxiety disorder that is characterized by uncontrollable worry about everyday things. The frequency, intensity, and duration of the worry are disproportionate to the actual source of worry, and such worry often interferes with daily functioning.
Acrophobia	Acrophobia is an extreme or irrational fear of heights. It belongs to a category of specific phobias, called space and motion discomfort that share both similar etiology and options for treatment.
Agoraphobia	Agoraphobia is an anxiety disorder which primarily consists of the fear of experiencing a diffucult or embarrassing situation from which the sufferer cannot excape. As a result, severe sufferers of agoraphobia may become confined to their homes, experiencing difficulty traveling from this "safe place."
Claustrophobia	Claustrophobia is an anxiety disorder that involves the fear of enclosed or confined spaces. It may be accompanied by panic attacks in situations such as being in elevators, trains or aircraft.

OCD	Obsessive-compulsive disorder (OCD) is a mental disorder most commonly characterized by intrusive, repetitive thoughts resulting in compulsive behaviors and mental acts that the person feels driven to perform, according to rules that must be applied rigidly, aimed at preventing some imagined dreaded event. In severe cases, it affects a person"s ability to function in every day activities. The disorder is often debilitating to the sufferer"s quality of life.
Taijin kyofusho	Taijin kyofusho is a Japanese and Korean culture-specific syndrome, Culture-Bound Syndrome.
Major depressive disorder	The diagnosis of a major depressive disorder occurs when an individual experiences a major depressive episode and depressed characteristics, such as lethargy and depression, last for 2 weeks or longer and daily functioning becomes impaired.
Anger	Anger is a an emotion. It is a psychophysiological response to pain, perceived suffering or distress, or threat thereof, which has been uncalled for or unjustly brought upon oneself or others, at least from a subjective viewpoint. A threat may be real, discussed, or imagined.
Learned helplessness	Learned helplessness is a psychological condition in which a human being or an animal has learned to believe that a situation is helpless. It has come to believe that it has no control over its situation and that whatever it does is futile. As a result, the human being or the animal will stay passive in the face of an unpleasant, harmful or damaging situation, even when it does actually have the power to change its circumstances.
Lithium	Lithium salts are used as mood stabilizing drugs primarily in the treatment of bipolar disorder, depression, and mania; but also in treating schizophrenia. Lithium is widely distributed in the central nervous system and interacts with a number of neurotransmitters and receptors, decreasing noradrenaline release and increasing serotonin synthesis.
Suicide prevention centers	Suicide prevention centers assume that people are often ambivalent about taking their own lives. These centers are staffed primarily by paraprofessionals who are trained to be empathic and to encourage suicidal callers to consider nondestructive ways of dealing with life issues.
Depressive explanatory style	A habitual tendency to attribute negative events to causes that are stable, global, and internal is called a depressive explanatory style.
Jerusalem syndrome	The Jerusalem syndrome is a group of mental phenomena involving the presence of either religiously themed obsessive ideas, delusions or other psychosis-like experiences that are triggered by a visit to the city of Jerusalem. It is not endemic to one single religion or denomination but has affected Jews and Christians of many different backgrounds. The best known, although not the most prevalent, manifestation of the Jerusalem syndrome is the phenomenon whereby a person who seems previously balanced and devoid of any signs of psychopathology becomes psychotic after arriving in Jerusalem.
Dissociative identity disorder	Dissociative Identity Disorder, as defined by the American Psychiatric Association"s Diagnostic and Statistical Manual of Mental Disorders, is a mental condition whereby a single individual evidences two or more distinct identities or personalities, each with its own pattern of perceiving and interacting with the environment.

Word salad	Word salad is a string of words that vaguely resemble language, and may or may not be grammatically correct, but is utterly meaningless.
Delusions of grandeur	Delusions of grandeur are a false belief that one is a famous person or a person who has some great knowledge, ability, or authority.
Reactive schizophrenia	Reactive schizophrenia is characterized by rapid onset, presence of a precipitating stressor, with associated social adequacy and volatile and intense emotional expression.
Disorganized schizophrenia	Disorganized schizophrenia is a subtype of schizophrenia. This type is characterized by prominent disorganized behavior and speech, and flat or inappropriate emotion and affect.
Paranoid schizophrenia	Paranoid schizophrenia is a type of schizophrenia characterized primarily by delusions-commonly of persecution-and by vivid hallucinations .
Process schizophrenia	Process schizophrenia has a slow onset, a lack of a precipitating stressor, typically with associated social skill deficits and flat affect.
Residual schizophrenia	Residual schizophrenia is a diagnosis given to patients who have had an episode of schizophrenia but who currently do not show psychotic symptoms, but do show signs of the disorder.
Undifferentiated schizophrenia	A type of schizophrenia that is characterized by disorganized behavior, hallucinations, delusions, and incoherence is an undifferentiated schizophrenia.
Depersonalization disorder	Depersonalization Disorder is a dissociative disorder in which sufferers are affected by persistent or recurrent feelings of depersonalization. The symptoms include a sense of automation, feeling a disconnection from one"s body, and difficulty relating oneself to reality.
Dissociative amnesia	Dissociative Amnesia is related to trauma or general psychological disorientation. It is not the result of specific brain injury or disease.
Dissociative fugue	Dissociative fugue is a state of mind where a person experiences a dissociative break in identity and attempts to run away from some perceived threat, usually something abstract such as the person"s identity. People who enter into a fugue state may disappear, running away to a completely different geographical region, in unplanned travel, and assuming another identity.
Antisocial personality disorder	Antisocial personality disorder is a psychiatric condition characterized by an individual"s common disregard for social rules, norms, and cultural codes, as well as impulsive behavior, and indifference to the rights and feelings of others.
Borderline personality disorder	Borderline personality disorder is a psychiatric diagnosis in the Diagnostic and Statistical Manual of Mental Disorders (DSM-IV Personality Disorders 301.83) that describes a prolonged disturbance of personality function characterized by depth and variability of moods. The disorder typically involves unusual levels of instability in mood; "black and white" thinking, or "splitting"; chaotic and unstable interpersonal relationships, self-image, identity, and behavior; as well as a disturbance in the individual"s sense of self. In extreme cases, this disturbance in the sense of self can lead to periods of dissociation.

Insight therapy	Insight therapy is the treatment of a personality disorder by attempting to uncover the hidden causes of the individual"s problem and to assist in the elimination of defense mechanisms. Some examples of insight therapy include psychodynamic and humanistic therapies.
Free association	In psychoanalysis, the uncensored uttering of all thoughts that come to mind is called free association. In it, patients are asked to continually relate anything which comes into their minds, regardless of how superficially unimportant or potentially embarrassing the memory threatens to be.
Interpretation	In logic, an Interpretation is a function that provides the extension of symbols and strings of symbols of an object language. For example, an Interpretation function could take the predicate T (for "tall") and assign it the extension {a} (for "Abraham Lincoln"), signifying that under this function Abraham Lincoln is considered tall. The object language which is being interpreted is typically a formal language, i.e. a mere set of strings of symbols.
Interpersonal therapy	Interpersonal therapy is a time-limited psychotherapy that was developed as an outpatient treatment for adults who were diagnosed with moderate or severe non-delusional depression. Interpersonal therapy was first developed as a theoretical placebo for the use in psychotherapy research by Gerald Klerman, et al. IPT was, however, found to be quite effective in the treatment of several psychological problems.
Cognitive restructuring	.Cognitive restructuring in cognitive therapy is the process of learning to refute cognitive distortions, or fundamental "faulty thinking," with the goal of replacing one"s irrational, counter-factual beliefs with more accurate and beneficial ones.
Intrapersonal communication	Intrapersonal communication is language use or thought internal to the communicator.
Cognitive-behavior therapy	Cognitive-Behavior Therapy is a psychotherapy based on cognitions, assumptions, beliefs, and behaviors, with the aim of influencing disturbed emotions. The general approach, developed out of behavior modification, Cognitive Therapy and Rational Emotive Behavior Therapy, has become widely used to treat various kinds of neuroses and psychopathology, including mood disorders and anxiety disorders.
All-or-nothing thinking	Classifying things in black-and-white terms is called all-or-nothing thinking.
Hasty generalization	Hasty generalization is a logical fallacy of faulty generalization by reaching an inductive generalization based on insufficient evidence. It commonly involves basing a broad conclusion upon the statistics of a survey of a small group that fails to sufficiently represent the whole population. Its opposite fallacy is called slothful induction, or denying the logical conclusion of an inductive argument (i.e. "it was just a coincidence".)
Selective perception	Selective perception may refer to any number of cognitive biases in psychology related to the way expectations affect perception. Selective perception are of two types Low level - Perceptual vigilance and High level- Perceptual defense.
Client-centered therapy	Client-centered therapy was developed by the humanist psychologist Carl Rogers in the 1940s and 1950s. He referred to it as counseling rather than psychotherapy.
Active listening	Active listening is an intent to "listening for meaning" in which the listener checks with the speaker to see that a statement has been correctly heard and understood. The goal of active listening is to improve mutual understanding.

Alcoholics Anonymous	The primary purpose of Alcoholics Anonymous membership is to stay sober and help others do the same. It. formed the original twelve-step program and has been the source and model for all similar recovery groups.
Group therapy	Group therapy is a form of psychotherapy during which one or several therapists treat a small group of clients together as a group. This may be more cost effective than individual therapy, and possibly even more effective.
List of self-help organizations	This is a list of self-help organizations Recovery programs using Alcoholics Anonymous" twelve steps and twelve traditions either in their original form or by changing only the alcohol-specific references: · Alcoholics Anonymous (AA) · Emotions Anonymous (EA) · Marijuana Anonymous · Narcotics Anonymous (NA) · Sexaholics Anonymous (SA) · Rational Recovery · Narconon · Recovery International (formerly Recovery, Inc.) · GROW · Toastmasters International · Self-help (law) · Self-help group (finance) · Do it yourself · Kisumu Links Self Help Group .
Behavioral rehearsal	Behavior therapy technique in which the client practices coping with troublesome or anxiety arousing situations in a safe and supervised situation is a behavioral rehearsal.
Relationship counseling	Relationship counseling is the process of counseling the parties of a relationship in an effort to recognize and to better manage or reconcile troublesome differences and repeating patterns of distress. The relationship involved may be between members of a family, couples, employees or employers in a workplace, or between a professional and a client.
Family therapy	Family therapy is a branch of psychotherapy that works with families and couples in intimate relationships to nurture change and development. It tends to view these in terms of the systems of interaction between family members. It emphasizes family relationships as an important factor in psychological health.

95

Aversion therapy	Aversion therapy is a form of psychiatric or psychological treatment in which the patient is exposed to a stimulus while simultaneously being subjected to some form of discomfort. This conditioning is intended to cause the patient to associate the stimulus with unpleasant sensations, and to then stop a certain behavior.
Systematic desensitization	Systematic desensitization is a type of behavioral therapy used in the field of psychology to help effectively overcome phobias and other anxiety disorders. More specifically, it is a type of Pavlovian therapy developed by a South African psychiatrist, Joseph Wolpe. To begin the process of systematic desensitization, one must first be taught relaxation skills in order to control fear and anxiety responses to specific phobias.
Virtual reality therapy	Virtual reality therapy is a method of psychotherapy that uses virtual reality technology to treat patients with anxiety disorders, post traumatic stress disorder, and several other medical phobias. New technology also allows for the treatment of addictions. The first research for virtual reality therapy was done in the early 1990s.
Test anxiety	High levels of arousal and worry that seriously impair test performance is referred to as test anxiety.
Modeling therapy	Modeling therapy is a therapeutic approach to phobias in which the person with the phobia observes a model in the act of coping with, or responding appropriately in the fear-producing situation.
Participant modeling	A behavior therapy in which an appropriate response is modeled in graduated steps and the client attempts each step, encouraged and supported by the therapist is participant modeling.
Antianxiety drugs	Drugs that can reduce a person's level of excitability while increasing feelings of well-being are called antianxiety drugs.
Biomedical therapy	Biomedical therapy is a form of treatment that relies on drugs andother medical procedures to improve psychological functioning. Biomedical therapy includes Psychopharmacology, Electroconvulsive Treatment, and Psychosurgery.
Monoamine oxidase inhibitors	Monoamine oxidase inhibitors are a group of antidepressant drugs that prevent the enzyme monoamine oxidase from deactivating neurotransmitters of the central nervous system.
Neuroleptics	Neuroleptics are a group of drugs used to treat psychosis. Common conditions with which neuroleptics might be used include schizophrenia, mania and delusional disorder. They also have some effects as mood stabilizers, leading to their frequent use in treating mood disorder (particularly bipolar disorder) even when no signs of psychosis are present.
Psychopharmacology	Psychopharmacology refers to the study of the effects of drugs on the mind and on behavior; also known as medication and drug therapy.
Selective serotonin reuptake inhibitors	Selective serotonin reuptake inhibitors or serotonin-specific reuptake inhibitor are a class of compounds typically used as antidepressants in the treatment of depression, anxiety disorders, and some personality disorders. They are also typically effective and used in treating premature ejaculation problems as well as some cases of insomnia. Selective serotonin reuptake inhibitors increase the extracellular level of the neurotransmitter serotonin by inhibiting its reuptake into the presynaptic cell, increasing the level of serotonin available to bind to the postsynaptic receptor.

Tricyclic antidepressants	Tricyclic antidepressants (TCAs) are a class of psychoactive drugs used primarily as antidepressants which were first introduced in the early 1950s. They are named after their chemical structure, which contains three rings of atoms. They are closely related to the tetracyclic antidepressants (TeCAs), which contain four rings of atoms.
Fluoxetine	Fluoxetine is an antidepressant of the selective serotonin reuptake inhibitor class. It is approved for the treatment of clinical depression, obsessive-compulsive disorder, bulimia nervosa, panic disorder and premenstrual dysphoric disorder.
Electroconvulsive therapy	Electroconvulsive therapy, is a controversial psychiatric treatment in which seizures are induced with electricity for therapeutic effect. It is often used as a treatment for severe major depression which has not responded to other treatment, and is also used in the treatment of mania, catatonia, schizophrenia and other disorders.
Lobotomy	A lobotomy is a form of psychosurgery that consists of cutting the connections to and from, or simply destroying, the prefrontal cortex. These procedures often result in major personality changes and possible mental disabilities. This method was used in the past to treat a wide range of severe mental illnesses, including schizophrenia, clinical depression, and various anxiety disorders. After the introduction of the antipsychotic Thorazine, this form of psychosurgery fell out of common use.
Psychosurgery	Psychosurgery is a term for surgeries of the brain or autonomic nervous system involving the severance of neural pathways to effect a change in behavior, usually to treat or alleviate severe mental illness. The procedures typically considered psychosurgery are now almost universally shunned as inappropriate, due in part to the emergence of less-invasive methods of treatment such as psychiatric medication.
Tardive dyskinesia	Tardive dyskinesia is a neurological disorder caused by the long-term or high-dose use of dopamine antagonists, usually antipsychotics. Tardive dyskinesia is characterized by repetitive, involuntary, purposeless movements. Features of the disorder may include grimacing, tongue protrusion, lip smacking, puckering and pursing of the lips, and rapid eye blinking.
Psychedelics	Psychedelics are psychoactive drugs whose primary action is to alter the thought processes of the brain and perception of the mind. It is part of a wider class sometimes known as the hallucinogens, which also includes related substances such as dissociatives and deliriants.
Poverty	Poverty is the condition of lacking economic access to fundamental human needs such as food, shelter and safe drinking water. While some define poverty primarily in economic terms, others consider social and political arrangements to be intrinsic.
Institutionalization	The term _Institutionalization_ is widely used in social theory to denote the process of making something (for example a concept, a social role, particular values and norms, or modes of behaviour) become embedded within an organization, social system, or society as an established custom or norm within that system. The term "_Institutionalization_" may also be used to refer to the committing by a society of an individual to a particular institution such as a mental institution.

Involuntary commitment	Involuntary commitment is the practice of using legal means or forms as part of a mental health law to commit a person to a mental hospital, insane asylum or psychiatric ward against their will or over their protests. Involuntary commitment is used to some degree for each of the following headings although different jurisdictions have different criteria. Some allow involuntary commitment only if the person both appears to be suffering from a mental illness and that the effects of this produce a risk to themselves or others.
Deinstitutionalization	The transfer of former mental patients from institutions into the community is referred to as deinstitutionalization.
Meta-analysis	In statistics, a meta-analysis combines the results of several studies that address a set of related research hypotheses. The first meta-analysis was performed by Karl Pearson in 1904, in an attempt to overcome the problem of reduced statistical power in studies with small sample sizes; analyzing the results from a group of studies can allow more accurate data analysis.

LaVergne, TN USA
23 September 2010
198008LV00002B/235/P

9 781616 541965